Healing America's Wounds is a timely prophetic word that will make a difference. By reading this book not only will you be changed, but through you, also our land.

Loren Cunningham, President, Youth With a Mission

■ ■ ■

The quicker you read *Healing America's Wounds*, the sooner you can be a part of the application of its powerful message. Please read it today.

Dick Eastman, International President, Every Home for Christ, Chairman, America's National Prayer Committee

■ ■ ■

God has placed in John Dawson's spirit a redemptive power, a special grace. If the Church sets in motion the truths contained in this book, a major step toward healing our national wounds shall be attained.

Francis Frangipane, River of Life Ministries

■ ■ ■

What a gift is John Dawson to the Body of Christ! One of our most lucid Christian authors, John writes with prophetic insight and wisdom, challenging us to see that repentance and reconciliation is not just an individual matter, but one of significance in the healing of nations. A must-read book.

Chuck Girard, Christian Recording Artist

■ ■ ■

In *Healing America's Wounds*, John Dawson uncovers the source of our national wounds, then points toward the only hope of reconciliation. No message is more urgently needed.

Steve Green, Christian Recording Artist

■ ■ ■

This book was written by the hand of John Dawson, but it flows from the heart of God. It will enlighten you, challenge you, and make you cry. As you read, your heart will be broken for the wounds of America and, at the same time, stirred and challenged to be agents of healing as followers of Jesus.

Jane Hansen, International President, Women's AGLOW Fellowship International

John Dawson is one of the brightest, spiritually reliable and morally trustworthy young men in the rising generation of spiritual leaders. His penetrating insights provide us with practical pathways to take spiritual action.

Jack W. Hayford, Senior Pastor, The Church On The Way

■ ■ ■

As an American, I grieve over the wounds that have been inflicted upon our nation. As a Christian, this book reminds me that we are all to be agents of healing in the hands of the Master Physician.

Dallas Holm, Christian Recording Artist

■ ■ ■

Healing America's Wounds is more than theory, it is solid biblical truth addressing some of the ultimate issues of our times. I believe that John Dawson has produced another landmark book to help the Church focus on her mandate for this hour.

Rick Joyner, MorningStar Publications

■ ■ ■

A penetrating audit of American life that sneaks behind our blinders. It's like an eye-opening modern walk to Emmaus with the Lord.

Samuel Hugh Moffett, Professor of Ecumenics and Mission, Emeritus, Princeton Theological Seminary

■ ■ ■

Healing America's Wounds is a very important book. It not only shows us where we started and where we've gone wrong, but also *what to do about it and how to do it.*

Jimmy and Carol Owens, Songwriters

■ ■ ■

Healing America's Wounds could not have come at a better time in our history. Both racism and classism are again on the rise. Our country is experiencing a desperate need for leadership and direction that would give insight into healing its recent and historical wounds. John Dawson's new book could be a new beginning for Christianity in America.

John Perkins, Founder, Voice of Calvary Ministries
Publisher, URBAN FAMILY Magazine

In *Healing America's Wounds*, New Zealand-born John Dawson opens our eyes as Americans to the source of our own pain, fear and prejudice. More importantly he helps us in practical ways to arrive at solutions for society and the Church. Be prepared to see history in a very different light...and be challenged to rethink, repent and be renewed.

The Rt. Rev. John-David Schofield, Bishop, The Episcopal Diocese of San Joaquin, California

■ ■ ■

This could easily be the most important message of the decade. May God give each of us the courage to embrace it—and boldly live it out!

Melody Green Sievright, President, Last Days Ministries

■ ■ ■

Every once in a while a book comes along that reshapes the spiritual landscape of the world for the better due to the timely message the Holy Spirit chooses to convey through it. *Healing America's Wounds* is such a book. It is an absolute must for anyone involved in reaching cities for Christ.

Reverend Ed Silvoso, President, Harvest Evangelism

■ ■ ■

As a Sioux Indian and pastor, I wept while reading this book because for the first time I see Native Americans being recognized as a needed and significant part of the church in America. John Dawson is a prophetic voice not leaving any of us "blameless" for our nation's fragmented condition. As the "host" people of this great land we are willing to again welcome our white brethren, release our bitterness, forgive centuries of neglect and injustice, and join with you in healing America's wounds.

Richard Twiss, Senior Pastor, New Discovery Community Church Executive Director, North American Native Christian Council

■ ■ ■

John Dawson has provided us another foundational, cutting-edge textbook for advancing God's kingdom! *Healing America's Wounds* has all the marks of a classic. I feel that my students would be disadvantaged in their ministry if they did not read, digest and boldly act upon the principles of this book.

C. Peter Wagner, Fuller Theological Seminary

JOHN DAWSON

AUTHOR OF THE BEST-SELLING TAKING OUR CITIES FOR GOD

HEALING AMERICA'S WOUNDS

Regal Books
A Division of Gospel Light
Ventura, California, U.S.A.

Published by Regal Books
A Division of Gospel Light
Ventura, California, U.S.A.
Printed in U.S.A.

Regal Books is a ministry of Gospel Light, an evangelical Christian publisher dedicated to serving the local church. We believe God's vision for Gospel Light is to provide church leaders with biblical, user-friendly materials that will help them evangelize, disciple and minister to children, youth and families.

It is our prayer that this Regal Book will help you discover biblical truth for your own life and help you meet the needs of others. May God richly bless you.

For a free catalog of resources from Regal Books/Gospel Light please contact your Christian supplier or call 1-800-4-GOSPEL.

Library of Congress Cataloging-in-Publication Data
Dawson, John, 1951-
    Healing America's wounds : discovering our destiny / John Dawson
        p. cm.
    ISBN 0-8307-1692-0
    1. United States—Religion—1960- 2. Repentance—Christianity. 3. Evangelistic work—United States.   I. Title.
BR526.D38   1994   94-7170
277.3'0829—dc20   CIP

1 2 3 4 5 6 7 8 9 10 11 12 13 14 / 02 01 00 99 98 97 96 95 94

Rights for publishing this book in other languages are contracted by Gospel Literature International (GLINT). GLINT also provides technical help for the adaptation, translation and publishing of Bible study resources and books in scores of languages worldwide. For further information, contact GLINT, P.O. Box 4060, Ontario, CA 91761-1003, U.S.A., or the publisher.

To the shepherds, the peacemakers
and those who pray.

■ ■ ■

CONTENTS

■

Part III
Repairer of the Breach

■ ■ ■

I wish to thank the Americans, from the boardroom to the barrio, who have received me without prejudice, told me their story and taught me these things.

. . .

Preface

SOMETHING'S HAPPENING!

It's not like an earthquake. It's more like being lifted by the tide, a surging tide of God's grace. Across the world, the new decade is marked by the emergence of citywide prayer meetings.

Some of the largest pastoral prayer meetings in United States history have recently taken place. In the last few months, I have traveled to 13 other countries that are also experiencing the same phenomena.

What is God up to? We can only wonder at His tactics, but His motives are clear enough. He loves us. He has not abandoned our generation. He governs in the affairs of people and nations, and He is setting the stage for harvest.

Amidst the terrifying realities and awesome potentials of the world at the beginning of the twenty-first century, it is no surprise that God is drawing His Church into the communion of prayer. I do not see prayer as man acting upon God, but God acting upon man. It is Jesus expressing His own ministry of intercession through those He has drawn and energized by His

Spirit. It is Jesus the Discipler of nations, Jesus the Lord of the harvest, Jesus the Captain of the heavenly host, Jesus the Head of the Church.

Now more than ever we need Jesus, the Master Teacher, to give us His mind. I for one sense the poverty of my understanding, but I know that God will give His wisdom as we take the next step of obedience. He gives us daily direction and we trust that eternal destiny is being worked out through our simple response to His grace.

The whole of human history is merely the backdrop for the revelation of His matchless nature and character. Our generation, like all others, includes those serving a brief earthly apprenticeship for eternity. Like the redeemed of all generations, we walk in simple faith knowing, "He who began a good work in you will perfect it" (Phil. 1:6).

The Melchizedek Factor

Abraham's faith amazes me. God called him out of a pagan culture. He did not have the Scriptures to guide him. Abraham was ignorant of so much compared with us—we who can hold Genesis through Revelation in one hand—yet he came to know God and to trust Him fully.

Imagine Abraham's feelings when Melchizedek walked away. This mysterious priest/king, described in Genesis 14, represented a connection to the eternal and the answer to a myriad of unanswered questions.

In a sense we still walk like Abraham. We do not know the true nature of the universe or what it means to rule with Christ in eternity, but we do know God as a person. He has revealed Himself in Jesus and that is more than enough for this brief pilgrimage.

In the past few months, the reality of God's sovereignty

in human history has filled me with wonder. It's true that we are in the midst of judgment; however, God continues to work His redemptive purpose.

In the following pages, I hope to encourage you with the promises of a heavenly Father who not only cleanses and heals the individual, but also heals the wounded spirit of nations.

Out of the experience of the prayer movements of Los Angeles came the teaching on intercession covered in my book *Taking Our Cities for God* (Creation House, 1989). A work described by C. Peter Wagner as, "The first textbook-quality treatment of strategic-level spiritual warfare to appear."

I did not write such a book to suggest an ecclesiastical takeover of our cities in a governmental sense, or even that Christian action can completely halt the institutional and personal evil of those who have rejected Christ. *Taking Our Cities for God* explored the implications of prayer at the cosmic level. What happens when we pray? What does the Bible reveal about the victory of Jesus over the devil? Why is united prayer so important?

The book now in your hand is a companion volume, so I will not attempt to go over that ground again, instead we will take an in-depth look at one important facet of God's grace. I have come to call this facet "identificational repentance." In the three years since the publication of *Taking Our Cities for God*, I have attended and spoken at citywide prayer gatherings in more than 90 cities in the United States. I want to share with you what I have learned and experienced in the hope that it will encourage you and cause God to be praised.

This book is partly a report on what God is doing, partly a journey of personal discovery of God's grace. All over the world, tears of repentance are flowing. This is a day of God's merciful visitation. Let's respond to Jesus. It's time to get involved.

- - -

PART
I

HOPE IN THE MIDST
OF JUDGMENT

*"For I will restore you to health and
I will heal you of your wounds,"
declares the Lord, "Because they
have called you an outcast, saying:
'It is Zion; no one cares for her.'"*

Jeremiah 30:17

1

L.A. Is
Burning!

*"Therefore, the Lord has kept the calamity
in store and brought it on us."*

Daniel 9:14

Black night shrouds the empty freeway. An irritating whine can
be heard in the distance, coming closer. Now we hear it, the
growl of high-revving engines and the shriek of sirens. Rodney
King's sedan is howling north on the 210 freeway, the Los Angeles Police Department in hot pursuit.

The intensity of light and sound draws Mr. Holliday to his
window. In a town jaded by the constant sound of sirens, he
stands watching the scene on the street below; his fascination
turns to horror. He grasps his video camera and switches it on.

We all saw what he saw. On the television screens of the
wide world. Beating, hitting, slugging. We saw it repeatedly on
every news channel in Los Angeles, 56 crashing, bone-jarring

blows. Like a nightmare, the shadowy images on the screen battered down the shreds of goodwill remaining between the LAPD and the black community.

I'm standing on that spot right now, scratch pad in hand, writing to you. It's strange to think that the greatest civil unrest since the Civil War should have erupted from this mundane piece of dirt and weeds, just down the street from my house. The actions of a handful of people on March 3, 1991, touched a vast bruise in the American soul and set off a shock wave of protest, violence and looting that took 59 lives here in Los Angeles, devalued property by billions of dollars and triggered rioting in major cities from coast to coast.

On April 28, 1992, following the not-guilty verdict in the trial of four white officers from our local police station, a peaceful candlelight vigil was held right here. Afterward, thugs and gang members began to loot two nearby stores. A roving crowd of about 200 began to break windows and loot stores in the surrounding communities of Pacoima, Arleta and Panorama City. Ralphs market where Julie and I shop was saved by its butchers, who stood in the doorways threatening the mob with their meat cleavers. A few miles away, the central part of Los Angeles entered into three days of terror.

What we saw was appalling. For more than 20 years, my wife, Julie, and I had been part of those working and praying for revival and racial reconciliation. The enormous racial diversity of Los Angeles had always sparked in us a hopeful vision of the future and now it was literally going up in flames, our worst nightmares surpassed.

Angelinos experienced the brutality of mob rule. Parts of the city virtually ceased to function. Hundreds of thousands of citizens were sent home from schools, offices and public facilities, and all sporting events were suspended; 3,700 fires raged out of control over a wide area. This, along with vandalism during looting, destroyed or damaged more than 5,000 buildings.

National guardsmen and federal troops began to pour into our neighborhoods because city police were totally overwhelmed. Worst of all, like a mirror-image replay of the King beating, was the live television broadcast of the assault on a white truck driver, Reginald Denny.

Pulled from his truck by at least five black men, he was battered into semiconsciousness with a five-pound oxygenator, punched and robbed. Soaked in blood and calling for help, he was repeatedly hit by beer bottles, kicked in the head and beaten with a claw hammer and a piece of concrete. He was finally rescued by four black bystanders and taken to a hospital where he underwent four hours of brain surgery.

> I BELIEVE THAT GOD HAS ALWAYS WANTED TO MAKE A PROPHETIC STATEMENT THROUGH THE AMERICAN CHURCH IN THE MIDST OF A WORLD HOPELESSLY STUCK IN ANCIENT ANIMOSITIES.

Under curfew each night, we huddled in front of the TV with our boys, hardly able to speak to each other about the numbing images of hatred, blood and flames flickering in front of us. Occasionally we would go to the balcony to observe the columns of smoke rising from points all across the city.

Friends called from as far away as Europe and Australia, worried for our safety, but a strange, grieving quietude had settled on our immediate neighborhood. Friends and neighbors for many years, our rainbow community mourned the misfortune of being at the center of such events.

We are described by the *Los Angeles Times* as, "A largely working-class racially mixed community where horse properties coexist with gangs and drugs, plagued by violent crime — some local, some spilling over from adjacent neighborhoods where gang members and drug dealers play cat-and-mouse with police."* We may look this way to an outsider, but in reality an intense community spirit exists in Lake View Terrace, a piece of Los Angeles where many neighbors have enjoyed deep and lasting friendship in an environment they love.

On the second evening of the riots, I found myself torn between the brutal images on TV and the vista of the burning city visible from my upstairs windows. I slumped at my desk and took up my Bible, desperate for God's encouragement. I found myself staring at the words of Hannah.

> "The bows of the mighty are shattered,
> but the feeble gird on strength....
> The Lord makes poor and rich;
> He brings low, He also exalts.
> He raises the poor from the dust,
> He lifts the needy from the ash heap"
> (1 Sam. 2:4,7,8).

In many ways, the black community is like Hannah. Tormented by her rival, she feels barren and rejected. "My lord, I am a woman of sorrowful spirit....Do not consider your maidservant a wicked woman, for out of the abundance of my complaint and grief I have spoken until now" (1 Sam. 1:15,16, *NKJV*).

That night, in spite of all the tragedy outside, I received a promise from God and my broken heart was filled with hope. I believe that as God gave Samuel to Hannah and thus restored the righteous foundations of Israel, He is bringing to birth a prophetic generation in the midst of the tears and torments of the black experience; that this unique people, placed by God at the heart of the American story, hold a key to our biggest national questions: Why is there an America? What is our

---

* Don Galpern, "Real Estate Experts Expect Riot to Harm Valley Market," Los Angeles Times, May 20, 1992.

national purpose to be? What is God up to with us?

I believe that God has always wanted to make a prophetic statement through the American Church in the midst of a world hopelessly stuck in ancient animosities. I believe that the dream in the heart of Jesus is to demonstrate a prototype of what has been considered impossible: All the cultures of the world reconciled to each other and serving one another with their gifts.

This is why racial injustice and rioting brings such humiliation to America in front of a watching world. It is not that we are worse than other nations, it is that we are violating our own redemptive purpose, thus releasing a wave of despair throughout all of humanity.

America's cities are now the greatest gatherings of ethnic and cultural diversity the world has ever seen. We have inherited the wounds of the world, the clash of ancient rivalries, and we have our own unfinished business, particularly with Native Americans and Afro-Americans.

Perhaps the greatest legacy of the riots of 1992 is a deepening sense of hopelessness. They came 28 years after the so-called Watts riots, which were also triggered by an incident of police brutality against a backdrop of frustration over joblessness and poverty. Nothing has changed. Everything is worse. The humanistic optimism of 1965 is totally discredited; the politician, educator and scientist have failed. Indeed, "the bows of the mighty are shattered" (1 Sam. 2:4).

Blacks and whites, Asians and Latinos, stare across the abyss that has opened at their feet. For blacks, the initial acquittal of the white police officers, and for whites the aftermath, tended to confirm each race's worst fears and suspicions about the other. Is there hope for reconciliation? Is there hope for our future? I believe so. Let me tell you a story from my native land.

■ ■ ■

2

I'M GUILTY, I ADMIT IT

A Prophetic Parable from a Distant Land

Now while I was speaking and praying, and confessing my sin and the sin of my people...

Daniel 9:20

New Zealand, summer of 1990. Sam stood at the front of the huge tent, held his guitar across his large chest and talked about God the Father. His broad, brown face seemed to embody everything that is beautiful and redemptive about the Polynesian race. As he began to lead us in worship, we in the crowd began to feel as though we were wrapped in the arms of God. I counted it a special privilege to be Sam's friend, and I thanked God with a full heart.

He paused between songs and told us a story. He talked of a Polynesian childhood in a European culture. It had been confusing. He talked about wounds of rejection and feelings of inferiority.

There was no bitterness in his voice. He just wanted to testify to God's grace. He wanted to tell us how God had healed his agonizing shyness and a debilitating speech impediment, a miracle that occurred the first time he was asked to share his faith in Jesus at a public meeting. *How could anybody hurt a beautiful person like Sam?* I thought.

Then he began to sing again, a song by John Pantry.

Wonderful grace
    that gives me the time to change.
Wonderful grace
    that lets me go free.
And all that I am
    and ever will be
I owe to the Savior
    who loves me.

Sam introduced me, and an atmosphere of reverent expectation settled on the crowd. I looked over the faces of my beloved countrymen, and such depth of emotion welled up inside me that I could hardly speak.

I talked about New Zealand—the Polynesian roots, the coming of the missionary, then the birth of a new nation only 150 years before that summer of 1990. I talked about a people of destiny so full of potential, yet wounded and limping, confused and bound. God creates nations (see Acts 17), yet the beautiful dream in His heart for New Zealand was so far from coming true.

Wounds of rejection, fear of authority, rebellion and independence, loneliness and isolation, fear of intimacy, withdrawal, melancholy, inferiority and addiction to false comforts—these were like livid scars marring our national face. How we had sinned against one another, race to race, management to labor, male to female, governor to governed, church to church.

As I spoke, a long-lost childhood memory began to haunt me. The crowd faded away and I was in grade school again. A new kid came to our class. His skin was brown and his school uniform was threadbare. He didn't fit in. We were white, middle-class city kids and he was a back-country Maori. We talked fast and knew our way around. He was lonely and confused. The kids picked on him, the teacher was impatient with him, he had no friend.

I was from a loving Christian home. My parents loved the Maori people, my unofficially adopted older brother was a Maori. All my compassion was aroused. I knew what to do. I should offer him friendship but I never moved across that room. I never joined him in the school yard. I seared my conscience. I just watched. Some of the kids mocked him because of his unusual name. His name was Wi. He soon left our school and I never saw him again.

Now standing in front of that huge crowd the full force of remorse filled my chest. I couldn't speak. I began to weep. Just a few minutes before I had wondered how anybody could have hurt Sam, yet I was no different than those who wounded him. Somewhere in New Zealand was a Maori man named Wi, just the same age as me, a man perhaps still deeply wounded by class and racial prejudice, a man who God once tried to love through a Christian white boy named John, but I chose pride. I chose my peers. I did not choose love.

Through my tears I confessed my actions. The Spirit of God was showing me that this was no small thing. I asked for forgiveness from every Maori present. I asked for God's forgiveness. I felt utterly ashamed.

Weeping began to spread through that huge crowd. Sam came up onto the platform and enveloped me in his huge arms. "Forgive me brother." I said.

"I forgive you," Sam said. And we both wept as the great grieving heart of God was revealed in our emotions.

It's as though the tears of many generations were poured out that day. There was no more preaching. Time did not matter. The Church of New Zealand was being held in the lap of the heavenly Father, and we wept like a grieving child until we had no more tears left to cry.

People streamed up to the microphone and unburdened their souls. Everybody was asking forgiveness of everybody. Painful things were brought into the open—the sins of our forefathers as well as the sins of today. The sins of men to women. Wounds between classes, races and cultures were healed.

God moved among us for two days, all day and into the night. It was similar to what happened to the Israelites long ago when God healed their land. "The descendents of Israel separated themselves from all foreigners, and stood and confessed their sins and the iniquities of their fathers" (Neh. 9:2).

That summer in New Zealand, the prayers of the saints of many generations began to be answered. We saw an outpouring of grace for repentance in five of the main cities and heard that the same phenomena was occurring in other cities throughout the land. Our team, which included Dale and David Garrett, pioneers of the contemporary praise movement, and Jackie Pullinger, a veteran missionary from Hong Kong, had never seen anything like it.

Could this take place in the cities of America?

It is taking place. When I returned to California, the first city I visited was Bakersfield. A large group of pastors was gathered in one of the historic black churches downtown. I noticed as they took their seats that the black pastors tended to sit to my right and the whites to my left; I thought it unusual to see such separation in a California city.

My heart was full of faith because of what I had experienced in New Zealand; so I explained the concept of identificational repentance, using portions of Daniel and Nehemiah as texts. I then gave them a report on what I had seen with my own eyes: auditoriums filled with weeping people; national wounds healed; the missing key to revival beginning to turn in an ancient, rusted lock.

I felt the Spirit of God asking me to give Him room, so I asked Him to move upon us and knelt down behind the wooden podium to wait. The silence was awful. Nothing happened. *It's not going to work here,* I thought as I eyed the exit longingly.

Then it happened. A man began weeping on the left side of the room. I peeked around the podium and I saw a well-dressed man with his head in his

> IF WE HAVE BROKEN OUR COVENANTS WITH GOD AND VIOLATED OUR RELATIONSHIPS WITH ONE ANOTHER, THE PATH TO RECONCILIATION MUST BEGIN WITH THE ACT OF CONFESSION.

hands, sobbing "Oh God, forgive us" many times. There was no tension or stridency, there seemed to be a united understanding of what was happening.

"Lord, I want to represent my vocation," he prayed. "We, as the city police department, have historically been such an instrument of rejection and injustice in our dealings with the black community. We have caused such wounding, such sorrow, please forgive me, please forgive us." And then to the black pastors: "I want to humble myself as a part of the police department. You have endured so much and, as a police officer who is a fellow believer, I want to ask for your forgiveness."

"We forgive you," came the gracious chorus of voices from all sides. Tears were flowing now. The sense of God's presence was palpable. It was such a simple thing to do, to say, yet foundation stones were moving in the heavenlies. You could feel it.

Since that day, I have seen and heard such things countless times. Pagan Americans are hopelessly trapped in old patterns of fear and distrust, but God's people are experiencing a season of grace for repentance and healing. This comes in the form of "godly sorrow" (see 2 Cor. 7:10).

The Punch Line

If we have broken our covenants with God and violated our relationships with one another, the path to reconciliation must begin with the act of confession. The greatest wounds in human history, the greatest injustices, have not happened through the acts of some individual perpetrator, rather through the institutions, systems, philosophies, cultures, religions and governments of mankind. Because of this, we, as individuals, are tempted to absolve ourselves of all individual responsibility.

Unless somebody identifies themselves with corporate entities, such as the nation of our citizenship, or the subculture of our ancestors, the act of honest confession will never take place. This leaves us in a world of injury and offense in which no corporate sin is ever acknowledged, reconciliation never begins and old hatreds deepen.

The followers of Jesus are to step into this impasse as agents of healing. Within our ranks are representatives of every category of humanity. Trembling in our heavenly Father's presence, we see clearly the sins of humankind and have no inclination to cover them up. Thus, we are called to live out the biblical practice of identificational repentance, a neglected truth that opens the floodgates of revival and brings healing to the nations. This is the subject we will explore in this book.

∎ ∎ ∎

Key Word Definition

Identification: As used in this book, signifies the act of con-sciously including oneself within an identifiable category of human beings.

3

TOOTH MARKS
ON THE BABY

Roots and Beginnings

*"Remember the former things long past, for
I am God, and there is no other."*

Isaiah 46:9

I did not encounter the common burrito until the age of 19. Of
course, this is not serious child abuse but it is a form of depri-
vation. Since that time, I have earnestly striven to redress this
deficit in the restaurants of east Los Angeles, and I have come to
thank God for all things Mexican.

Seriously, as I travel around the world, I see the beauty
of the nations. I'm not talking about scenery, I'm talking about
the unique personality of the nations. I see this most clearly
revealed in the international church. It is true that, in many
cases, European cultural forms have been inherited from missionaries, but the God-created personality of the peoples of the
earth shines right through.

Creation is more powerful than sin, more powerful than territorial spirits, more powerful than colonial legacies. If you have ever worshiped with Brazilians, you have experienced a joyous abandoned party in the presence of Jesus. The exuberance of carnival is redeemed; these people know how to celebrate being a child of God. I love the Italian commitment to family; I admire the dynamism of Nigerians and the hospitality of Egyptians; the nations are blessed with remarkable gifts — we need each other. There is no ideal world citizen or defining Christian personality: *Viva la différence!*

I am a missionary with Youth With a Mission (YWAM). To be a part of Youth With a Mission is to be adopted into a huge international family. For 23 years, I have walked in deep covenantal friendship with my coworkers from more than 100 countries. My fellow missionaries embody the redemptive traits of their mother cultures. They make me feel fabulously wealthy in terms of loving relationships.

I have just returned from our biannual strategy conference. This time it was held in New Delhi, India. Christian leaders from all over the subcontinent brought reports of their activities and gave us instruction. What a rich feast it was; it was an exhilarating glimpse of that day when the redeemed of every tribe, kindred and tongue gather around the risen Christ in grateful adoration.

Modern missionary enterprise is no longer a European/ American activity; it is the Latinos, Asians and Africans who are mobilizing in great numbers. The churches of the nations, when combined, bring us a picture of God's character and personality that cannot be accommodated in one language or represented adequately through one people.

One of the most moving moments of my life was the giant praise celebration that took place the night before the opening of the Los Angeles Olympics in 1984.

An expectant hush fell on the crowd. Sixteen thousand people leaned forward in excitement as the stadium infield filled with the flags of the nations. Hundreds of children from all over the world, dressed in national costumes, waved their banners in exaltation before the Lord. The next day, 11,000 Christian workers began their outreach, more than 2,000 of them foreigners, sent by God to minister in and to America. As the director of the outreach, I was in a position to hear repeatedly expressions of love and appreciation for America from believers from all around the world.

*"You Look Fabulous Darling"**

Americans have a distinct personality. To a foreigner like me, this is patently obvious. Americans living in the midst of this vastness of geography and population rarely see their own culture contrasted with others. They tend to be much more aware of difference *within* the land, evident in the racial characteristics of immigrant peoples. You need to know that the unifying American culture is a bulldozer. Immigrants like me quickly become so marked by it that we are seen as Americans by friends and relatives in our home countries in very short order.

What are these characteristics? Breadth of vision, communication skill, leadership, hospitality, generosity, flexibility, openness; my list is long. I am eternally grateful to Americans such as Loren Cunningham, founder of YWAM, a man with a heart the size of a bathtub and a vision as wide as the world. People such as Loren have made a place for me, opened doors for me and treated me with the utmost grace and generosity of spirit, in spite of my many flaws.

This is an embracing land, a place of healing, a place of new beginnings. However, I did not stumble into America as a refugee. I came from rich and beautiful New Zealand because of

---

* The immortal words of Billy Crystal.

my job. It was not my intention to settle here; that was one of God's surprises. However, my roots have gone deep in Los Angeles and here I will stay.

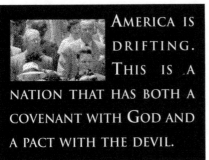

AMERICA IS DRIFTING. THIS IS A NATION THAT HAS BOTH A COVENANT WITH GOD AND A PACT WITH THE DEVIL.

America is a paradox. Large and loud, still brimming with promise; an exaggeration of the worst and best of the human condition. It is not my native land, but I love it. Being an urban missionary has exposed me to the dark side of America for 23 years, but I remain deeply committed to this nation. I am married to this land in more ways than one. My wife is an American and so are my three sons.

This is a nation with a tangled web of righteous and unrighteous roots. Over the years, the national self-concept has gradually changed from the Puritan-generated dream of a nation of servant ideals (e.g., refuge and outreach), to a nation dominated by conquest ideals (e.g., fame, wealth and power).

Lofty ideals were proclaimed at the time of our independence from Britain, but for most of our history Americans have valued unbridled liberty in the cause of personal success more than responsible servanthood. At present, the secular culture continues to turn away from idealism—such as we saw briefly in the '60s—toward the pursuit of affluence, security and status. Middle-class children are money-minded and career conscious. Hedonism rules our dreams. We are drifting. This is a nation that has both a covenant with God and a pact with the devil.

Something New on the Earth

America's roots fascinate me, particularly the European settlement of New England. The Pilgrims had a terrible ordeal in crossing the North Atlantic. One hundred and one men, women and children spent more than six weeks in the groaning hull of the *Mayflower*, enduring relentless storms.

Contrary to popular belief, the Pilgrims came as missionaries, not religious refugees seeking freedom of worship. They had already enjoyed 12 years of religious freedom in Holland. Bradford, Brewster and the others were separatists; Presbyterians who saw little hope of reforming the Church of England. They were persecuted by James I and they fled for their lives to Holland in 1607 and 1608. They did not come to New England seeking safety—they already had it. Their stated goal, according to William Bradford's diary, was to propagate the gospel among the Indians and to become stepping stones for the furtherance of the gospel to the uttermost parts of the earth, a dream that was realized when their great-grandchildren went west across the Pacific to Polynesia and beyond. This dream was not ethnocentric arrogance. They did not see Christianity as particularly English. Their own ancestors had been evangelized by Latin missionaries, coming from the east centuries before, and the Pilgrims understood that it was still the duty of Christians to bring salvation to distant peoples.

Having formed their own biblical commonwealth, based on the consent of the governed, the Pilgrims elected a deacon, John Carver, as the first New World governor, chosen by a free people in a free election. They were to pass on to the Puritans their form of government, which in turn was very little changed by the time the founding fathers established a national government 156 years later. The patriots of the Revolutionary War did not give us these values, they merely protected the continuance of a form of self-government practiced from the beginning.

The Puritans were also reformed in theology, but wanted to remain within the Church of England and to purify it. They were also persecuted. At the time of the great migration in the 1600s, 20,000 came to New England and 45,000 left England for the southern colonies and the Caribbean, which would be equivalent to the departure of more than 3 million people from

THE PURITANS SAW THE ATLANTIC AS THEIR RED SEA AND THEMSELVES AS A NEW ISRAEL IN THE WILDERNESS.

our current American population. They felt called to "complete" the Protestant Reformation, to live out its possibilities without molestation from governing authorities.

Luther and other reformers thought that the deliverance of Israel from Egypt was a type of the kind of journey that the individual believer takes from bondage to freedom in Christ. The Puritans began to apply this idea to their whole community. They saw the Atlantic as their Red Sea and themselves as a new Israel in the wilderness.

Providential Winds

The early colonies were established in an era of monumental change.

The emergence of England on the stage of colonization seemed touched with divine providence. Unusual personalities began to appear in the Elizabethan Age, such as Raleigh and Drake. Raleigh was an investor-adventurer, but Drake was animated by the religious zeal of one who saw Catholicism as apostate and Philip of Spain as its upholder.

During this time, the winds of Protestantism were sweeping Europe. Elizabeth established a Protestant church in 1559, as did Sweden. In Germany, the Reformers gained the upper hand, and in 1562 France was plunged into civil war. In the Netherlands, an alliance grew between Protestantism and aggrieved Dutch nobles chafing under Spanish rule.

Catholicism strove to dam back the tide threatening to engulf it by clarifying its own faith and resisting heresy by force. The instrument of battle, standing as the mainstay of the papacy, was the mightiest monarch in Christendom: Philip II of Spain. His nemesis was to become Francis Drake, the son of a poor Protestant preacher. I quote from Sugden, Drake's most recent biographer:

> Throughout his life, Drake's profound faith was arguably his most salient characteristic, and it provided the mainspring for his tempestuous career. There would be other motivations — patriotism, profit and personal grievance against the Spaniards — but none was greater than his Protestantism. Those who portray him purely as an avaricious free-booter have underestimated both the religious climate of the day and Drake's own intense piety. It was his confidence in God's protection and the belief that God worked through him that gave him the courage to brave the greatest dangers.[1]

On the eve of the Spanish Armada's expedition against England in 1588, Philip II ruled not only Spain, but also Portugal. He was the monarch of all permanent European settlements in the New World, the inheritor of the legacy of Columbus. A century later the English had entrenched themselves along the North Atlantic coast, from Maine to the Carolinas, and a great part of North America was lost bit by bit to Spanish domination.

Had the Duke of Medina Sidonia triumphed over Drake in the English Channel, had Spanish soldiers set foot in England, the character and history of North America most certainly would have taken on an entirely different shape. Its culture would have been Latin, not English; its religion Catholic, not

Protestant; its native races would have been exploited rather than ejected (although neither of these represent justice); its colonies would have been controlled by the centralized Spanish government rather than allowed to form a group of semi-independent, self-governing commonwealths. The impulse toward freedom would have been checked. Revolution against Spanish rule when it finally came would certainly not have produced the nation that emerged: a stable and flourishing republic, built upon the Anglo-American tradition of constitutional rights, representative government and civil liberties, that was largely the legacy of innovation in the church polity of the Protestant Reformation.

The Dutch, who were earnestly praying for an English victory over the Spanish Armada, were so impressed by the providential hand of God in the details of the great sea battle that they struck a coin bearing the words "Man purposeth, God disposeth, 1588." One side of the coin shows a sinking ship, while the other side reveals four men on their knees praying.

The Holy Experiment

The Puritans must have felt small on the world stage, yet so much was to come of their step into the New World. They were to model for the world and the nation ideas and values that are liberating peoples to this day. The Constitution of the United States is a secular expression of the Puritan's covenant with each other.

John Winthrop wrote down his vision of the new settlement while still aboard the *Arabella* on the Atlantic. He called it "A Model of Christian Charity." I quote in part:

> The Lord has given us leave to draw our own Articles. We shall find that the Lord will bless us when

we follow His counsel to love justice, love mercy and walk humbly with our God. If we are obedient to this covenant we can be sure that the Lord will bless us but if we neglect observance of these Articles the Lord will surely break out against us.[2]

The Articles centered on a deep commitment to care for one another. Through them, the Puritans tried to exemplify justice and mercy.

It is this covenantal aspect that fascinates me. It is certainly not unique to America (as most Americans think), but few other nations on earth have a governance so rooted in formally recorded statements that acknowledge God. Consider the Charter of Virginia, drawn up for the London Company in 1606.

I, James, by the grace of God, King of England, etc... defender of the faith...to deduce a colony of sundry of our people into that part of America, commonly known as Virginia...which may, by the providence of Almighty God, hereafter tend to the glory of His Divine Majesty, in propagating of Christian religion to such people...and may in time bring the infidels and savages, living in those parts, to human civility, and to a settled and quiet government.[3]

William Penn referred to Pennsylvania as a "holy experiment," and after independence many state constitutions were written, using even more explicit reference to God's supreme government and just, moral order. The preamble to the Massachusetts Constitution, adopted in 1790 reads:

We therefore, the people of Massachusetts, acknowledging, with grateful hearts, the goodness of the

Great Legislator of the Universe, in affording us, in the course of His providence, an opportunity, deliberately and peaceably, without fraud, violence, or surprise, of entering into an original, explicit, and solemn compact with each other; and for forming a new constitution of civil government, for ourselves and posterity; and devoutly imploring His direction in so interesting a design, do agree upon, ordain, and establish the following Declaration of Rights and Frame of Government, as the Constitution of the Commonwealth of Massachusetts.[4]

I have personally read the preambles to 47 of the states' constitutions. Each one openly expresses the idea of a covenant between people, made in the sight of God. The Puritans did indeed plant a seed that sprouted and bore fruit. Their influence on this nation can hardly be overstated, in education as well as in government. In 1636, Harvard University was founded on the motto:

Let every student be plainly instructed and earnestly pressed to consider well the main end of his life and studies is to know God and Jesus Christ which is eternal life, and therefore to lay Christ in the bottom as the only foundation of all sound knowledge and learning and seeing the Lord only giveth wisdom, let everyone seriously set himself to prayer in secret to seek it of Him.[5]

Prim and Proper Paranoids?

It is commonly believed today that the Puritans were self-righteous, neurotic prudes at best, and intolerant, sin-obsessed, witch-hunting bigots at worst. Not true. A reading of their records reveals not only basic English joviality, but also a deep joy in living, a culture given to regular celebrations. These are good roots, and all of today's immigrant peoples are blessed by them, but there is another side to the American story. Another dream was always competing with the Puritan ideal.

"And the dragon stood before the woman who was about to give birth, so that when she gave birth he might devour her child," says Revelation 12:4, a Scripture that exposes satanic strategy. At the birth of a child, a church or a nation, a need exists for vigilance in covering prayer because Satan would seek to wound and scar, to crack the foundation, to plant malignant seeds that will strangle and destroy when they are fully grown.

The Dark Side of the Story

First of all, dissension was present within Puritan ranks. The Massachusetts Bay Colony in particular became notorious for religious controversy and exclusivism, so beginning a series of spin-offs, such as Rhode Island, where the Puritan ideal was expressed in religious tolerance and inclusive government. In general, though, the Puritans enjoyed comparatively good relationships with each other and with the Indians. It was to the south, in Virginia, where a completely different experience was unfolding.

Reading the story of early Jamestown is similar to reading the list of curses in Deuteronomy 28. At the end of the first year, only 38 of the 104 settlers were still alive and the company that financed them eventually went bankrupt. This enterprise was founded on an entirely different set of values, primarily a desire for wealth and personal empowerment. In commenting on why men came to Virginia, Sir Walter Raleigh said that it was "to seek new worlds for gold, for praise, for glory."[6] One of the original Jamestown settlers, Captain John Smith, records that there was "no talke, no hope, nor worke, but dig gold, wash gold, refine gold, lode gold."[7] But no gold was found in Virginia.

The Virginia Company was comprised of London entrepreneurs who formed a joint stock company, a venture in which investors pooled their capital and shared the risks of business. From the beginning, there were bitter stockholders battles and struggles for company control in London, bitter disputes among the colonists and conflict with the Indians. In spite of the lack of gold, immigrants eventually began to pour in, drawn by cheap or free land and the profits that could be gained from an addictive weed named tobacco.

People continued to come to North America for religious reasons, such as Maryland's Catholics, but the vast majority pushed out toward the frontier, both north and south, driven by dreams of individual success.

The territory that is now the United States contained great diversity in the colonial period; Spanish friars, French backwoodsmen, Dutch merchants and Amerindian peoples, but it was the divide between northern and southern Anglos that eventually gave impetus to this nation's greatest wound: the Civil War. Although the English colonies were settled by people from the same culture speaking the same language, great differences existed between north and south.

The people of the north sought freedom to worship as they pleased. They clustered in small farming communities centered on the church, where they sought to win a living from the soil. They wanted a thrifty, independent, "godly" life. They were deeply committed to education. Grammar schools were established for all children of the colonies and a number of colleges date from this period.

The south was very different. In most cases the colonies were planted, not settled, by men of wealth and rank, who remained in Europe to reap the profits from their investments. The land was split into large estates, cultivated first by vagrants, paupers and felons from England and later by African slaves. The first slaves arrived in Jamestown as early as 1619. Religion in the south was paid lip service. It did not pervade society as it did in the north until the coming of the Methodist circuit riders in the years before the revolution.* Education was for the rich, and to obtain it they had to go north, or they had to employ northern tutors for their children. The vast mass of the people were ignorant. After all, how much formal education did you need to work in the fields?

This division between north and south proved to be the most dangerous crack in America's foundation. Even now, a web of less noticeable fractures wait for the day when sufficient stress will reveal them.

A Covenant People

You might think that all of this history is irrelevant; that God saves individuals and that human institutions, including the nation-state, are fallen, irredeemable and under the power of Satan. There is some truth in this, but it falls short of a biblical worldview.

The most famous theologian of the Great Awakening—a religious revival among the colonists—was Jonathan Edwards. He saw Americans as a covenant people; his text was 2 Chronicles 23:16: "Then Jehoiada made a covenant between himself and all the people and the king, that they should be the Lord's

---

*Methodism, along with the Jeffersonian school of Virginia deism, eventually paralleled the moral tradition of northern Calvinism and at times led the way. For instance, in the 1820s, the slave states contained a great many more antislavery societies than the free states and furnished leadership for the movement in the country. Sadly, by 1837, not one antislavery society remained in the whole south.

people." Edwards believed that the founding fathers could establish what he called a "federal covenant" with God and enjoy protection and "temporal blessings" as long as the covenant was honored. Let his words speak to us today.

> If a nation or people are very corrupt and remain obstinate in the evil way, God generally, if not universally, exercises these threatenings. God is more strict in punishing of a wicked people in this world than a wicked person. God often suffers particular persons that are to prosper in the world and discharges them to judgment in the world to come. But as a people we are punished only in this world. Therefore God will not suffer a people that grow very corrupt and refuse to be reclaimed, to go unpunished in this world.[8]

You may think this kind of thing took place only in the distant past. To the contrary, the idea has multiplied. Look at this remarkable statement made by President Chiluba of Zambia at State House in Lusaka on December 29, 1991. I quote in part:

> As you remember my first function after I was sworn in as the President of Zambia was to pray to my Heavenly Father. That was not just a part of the ceremony, but it was a prayer of thankfulness born out of my personal convictions that the change we have witnessed in Zambia in 1991 has only been possible because of the grace of God.
>
>   It is therefore only natural, that we have this solemn occasion here today, whereby I—on behalf of the Zambian nation—enter into a covenant with the one true God, whose love and saving grace is

revealed in God the Son, Jesus Christ.[9]

President Chiluba goes on to quote Jeremiah 7:23 *(NIV)*:

I gave them [Israel] this command: Obey me, and I
will be your God and you will be my people. Walk in
all the ways I command you, that it may go well with
you.

After further explanation of biblical texts and concepts,
the President concluded in prayer.

Dear God, as a nation we now come to Your throne
of grace, and we humble ourselves and admit our
guilt. We repent from all our wicked ways of idolatry,
witchcraft, the occult, immorality, injustice and corruption and all other sins that have violated Your
righteous laws. We turn away from all this and
renounce it all in Jesus' name. We ask for forgiveness and cleansing through the blood of Jesus.
Therefore we thank You that You will heal our land.
We pray that You will send healing, restoration,
revival, blessing and prosperity to Zambia. Amen.[10]

We're in This Together

It is natural for an African leader to identify with a group entity such as tribe or nation in this way, but our western civilization has its roots in the Greco-Roman world, a culture tending
toward a greater and greater emphasis on individualism. Carried
forward by the Renaissance and the Reformation, the privileges
and potentials of the individual are central to our values. We
even read the Bible this way. We as westerners see and empha-

size individual salvation and individual devotion to God, as well as individual rights and responsibilities.

For instance, we often take the book of Nehemiah and use it as a foundational text for the ministry of inner healing. That's not wrong. It's true that the restoration of the walls and gates of Jerusalem is an apt metaphor for the healing of an individual's personality. But we also need to apply this book to the subject it addresses, the architectural, social and spiritual restoration of a nation and its capital. Almost all of the Bible is written to corporate entities—to the seed of Abraham (ethnicity), the people of Israel (nationality), the citizens of Jerusalem (place) or the Christians of Rome (community). Even the book of Philemon addresses a corporate entity. It speaks to personal issues, but it is a letter from two people, Paul and Timothy, addressed to Philemon, Apphia, Archippus and to "the church in your house" (Philem. 1:2). As far as I can tell, that leaves the letters to Timothy and Titus as the only portions of the Bible written specifically to individuals.

> GOD DISCIPLES NATIONS, HE SHAPES NATIONS; THERE IS ALREADY A HISTORY OF GOD DEALING WITH THE NATION IN WHICH WE LIVE, WHETHER WE KNOW IT OR NOT.

Of course, God is committed to the individual, that we already know. But have we underestimated the degree to which God is dealing with us, as a people with historic continuity, just like Israel?

God is working in and through the agency of His redeemed children; however, He is not limited by that. For example, we see God's merciful hand in Somalia. Here is a nation that lost the privilege of self-government and came under the arbitrary control of United Nations forces. This is far from perfect, far from the dream in God's heart for that nation. Somalis lost their autonomy and experienced a military occupation, but it was the lesser of two evils given the awful suffering of the common people.

God rules sovereignly in the affairs of people and nations. He has not abdicated His Kingship over one square inch of this planet. Humankind sows to the whirlwind and reaps calamity. Peoples sacrifice to the idols of their own choosing, but God sees that they get the government they deserve. According to the level of internal moral restraint, external liberty is granted. If loving self-control is abandoned, then the discipline of ideologies or despots is what we are allowed to reap.*

"And it is He who changes the times and the epochs; He removes kings and establishes kings" (Dan. 2:21). It is God who claims to be the ultimate Creator of human diversity, including the nation-state.

> And He made from one, every nation of mankind to live on all the face of the earth, having determined their appointed times, and the boundaries of their habitation, that they should seek God, if perhaps they might grope for Him and find Him, though He is not far from each one of us (Acts 17:26,27).

God disciples nations, He shapes nations; there is already a history of God dealing with the nation in which we live, whether we know it or not.

---

*God is ultimately responsible for the preservation of the human race as a multigenerational biological unit. He, therefore, grants to individuals and nations moral freedom but not the freedom to endanger all of humanity.

He exercises governmental restraints on the liberty of a people to destroy their health, their environment and their immortal souls in a way that would trigger autogenocide on a global scale. Apparently the Molech-worshiping Canaanites were at this point of spiritual and biological contagion, leaving God with no alternative but to order their complete extinction at the hands of Joshua and the Hebrews.

Nehemiah was one who understood this. He had never seen Jerusalem. It was a distant city, spoken of by those of his parents' and grandparents' generations, but he understood the historic context of his own generation. He was part of a people group that had broken its covenants. His familiar surroundings were alien to his destiny, they represented judgment from God on His people and it was time to go back.

It is obvious that modern America has inherited both blessings and curses as a legacy from the past, but we do not understand what has happened to us as clearly as Nehemiah did. We, too, sense both captivity and loss, but we have forgotten who we are. Americans have a deep yearning to be part of a healthy nation doing good in the world, yet we are drifting into the future without purpose and without hope.

Our cities have become symbols of shame. How do we throw off the yoke of spiritual oppression and human injustice? How do we cleanse and heal the land? Do we concede the cities to principalities and powers; are they to be evermore empowered as contention and bitterness multiply indefinitely?

I have seen my city burning. Is that what our future is to be? The walls of our Jerusalem are broken down and our spiritual enemy has come through the gaps; what are we to do?

■ ■ ■

Recommended Reading:

Marshall, Peter, and Manuel, David. *The Light and the Glory.* Tarrytown, NY: Fleming H. Revell, 1980.

Notes
1. John Sugden, *Sir Francis Drake* (New York: Simon & Schuster, 1990), p. 7.

2. Quoted from "The American Vision, 360 Years Later" audiotape series, The American Vision Inc., Atlanta, GA.

3. Catherine Millard, *The Rewriting of America's History* (Camp Hill, PA: Christian Publications, 1991). Text is quoted from the 1991 report at Intercessors for America, Reston, VA.

4. Ibid.

5. "The American Vision" audiotape series.

6. Richard B. Morris, ed., and the editors of Time-Life Books, *The Life History of the United States*, Vol. I: Before 1775 (New York: Time-Life Books, 1963). Revised 1974 edition, p. 50.

7. Ibid.

8. Harvey S. Stoot, *Christian History* magazine, Vol. IV, No. 4.

9. David Shibley, Global Advance, May 1993.

10. Ibid.

4

BLOODSTAINS
ON THE GATES

Idolatry and Traumatization

Do not give the devil an opportunity.

Ephesians 4:27

Idolatry

Satanic power finds opportunistic access in two basic ways: idolatry and injustice. Acts of idolatry are designed to gain supernatural advantage, such as the sacrifice of babies to Molech in biblical times or the appeasement of the Aztec Sun God Huitzilopochtli by human sacrifice on the high altars of ancient Mexico. A one-sided bargain is struck with evil principalities by deceived peoples. Desperate for help, or perhaps just lusting for power, they give their allegiance to cruel gods and enter into a long enslavement that can only be broken by the atonement of Christ.

America's most common idol is mammon. This false god is served when an idolatrous trust is placed in the mode of exchange. Mammon's devotees show a ruthless desire for control over others through financial manipulation.

Individual initiative and private property are biblical freedoms that lead to the efficient production of goods and services, but the resulting wealth creates power and status, the lust for which becomes a snare. Many have built their altars here, desiring these more than a loving relationship with God and each other.

Injustice

The second opportunity for satanic access is found when people wound each other through selfish and unjust actions. Take, for example, father/daughter incest. The little girl is in no way responsible for her father's depraved actions, yet she is given a terrible wound to her soul and spirit. Anybody with a counseling ministry knows that this is a circumstance that tormenting spirits use to advantage. It's not fair, but then nothing satanic is fair. We have a jealous and cruel enemy who is filled with vindictive rage and will use any opportunity to separate us from our heavenly Father through the traumas of life.

Then we have the girl's father. A man who has seared his own conscience for a furtive moment of gratification. His intellect has been employed in justifying his dark fantasies, but once acted on, he finds himself rejected and accused by his own conscience. In this way, the oppressor becomes even more damaged than the oppressed. This is the phenomena we call guilt.

Guilt is really the ultimate wound of rejection. It is a harsh thing to be rejected by your mother or your spouse, but it is a more terrible thing to be rejected by yourself. To be condemned by your own conscience and intellect is to be tormented by an unquenchable flame. "Can a man take fire in his bosom, and his clothes not be burned?"(Prov. 6:27).

Every time this man sees his little girl he is reminded of his actions. She makes him feel bad, leading to an alienation that only deepens with time.

Now think of the implications for a nation. The human story is full of atrocities committed in the name of religious factions, ideologies, races and the nation-state itself. And, of course, Satan's greatest empowerment comes when some moral outrage is committed by those who invoke the name of Jesus. America grew out of Europe at a time when this condition was rampant.

The period following the Reformation saw Europe traumatized by shameful acts perpetuated by those claiming to serve both Reformed and Catholic causes. Europe is still haunted by these shadows. In France, the notorious Catherine de Médici became frantic when she supposed that her son King Charles IX had become the puppet of the Huguenot leader Coligny. She arranged for the assassination of Coligny, but the assassin only managed to wound him.

Becoming desperate, Catherine persuaded King Charles that Coligny was a traitor along with all Protestants and prepared a death list of Huguenot leaders. The political purge became a mass murder. Thousands of Protestants throughout France were butchered in one of the bloodiest episodes of the period, and France was once again tortured by religious civil war. In this case, the character of God was defamed before all peoples. Deep animosity was passed on to succeeding generations, and a spiritual darkness that is still evident today descended on France.

Genocide Is Contagious

Unless interrupted by healing grace, the atrocities of the past become ghosts within the memory of a people crying out for justice. Bitterness deepens and the victims often become tyrants, and so it multiplies. Let's look at an example.

The twentieth century's first holocaust took place, not in Nazi Germany, but in Turkish Armenia, where the government of the Ottoman Empire ordered a campaign of genocide against Armenian Christians. This tragedy has been largely forgotten in the west, obscured by the proximity of the greater scale of the Jewish holocaust, which began in Europe 30 years later.

In Armenian towns, the men were led away by the police, executed by a firing squad and thrown into mass graves or rivers. At the Kemakh Gorge, Kurds and troops of the Turkish 86th Calvary butchered more than 20,000 women and children. In Margada, in what is now the Syrian desert, 50,000 Armenians were killed over a period of several days. Starving, sick and naked families were roped together and pushed off a hill into the river. One person was shot so that the dead body would carry the others down and drown them. The killing reached its height in 1915, when more than one million men, women and children died.

> INJUSTICE OPENS THE DOOR FOR DEMONIC OPPRESSION, AN OPPRESSION THAT PEOPLE ARE POWERLESS TO DEAL WITH OUTSIDE OF THE CLEANSING, HEALING GRACE OF GOD.

The Armenian people have sought recognition for their holocaust for 70 years, but Turkey has never admitted its responsibility. There were no Nuremberg Trials, no restitution of rights and property, just a million and a half skeletons, whose very existence the Turks would later try to deny.

Today our television newscasts are showing us film of the corpses of Turkish Azeris: men, women and children allegedly massacred by Armenians in Nagorno-Karabakh, an autonomous region just east of Armenia. In our generation, the grievance continues. For these two peoples, the satanic stronghold of vengeful hatred lives on.

In Eastern Europe, Serbs justify a war conducted by rape, murder and starvation of whole cities by declaring themselves the injured party and wrapping themselves in self-pity. Belgrade television endlessly reminds the people of centuries of injury — the Serbs and the Croats massacred during the Hitler years, or those who died at the Battle of Kosovo in 1389, standing against the Muslims. Being a victim is the Rolls-Royce of self-justifications, and allows the brute killer to portray himself as the one to be pitied.

Current events are bad enough; however, the press daily reveals new information about the past, such as the recently opened KGB archives, which informed us that 1,400 Britains died in Soviet gulags following World War II.

The humanistic optimism of Western reporters is sometimes devastated by the reality of gross evil. During the Gulf War, I read this surprising statement from Kim Murphy, a *Los Angeles Times* reporter, on location in Kuwait City.

> That night, I remember looking out over the eerily dark city and remembering the horrors that had been visited upon it for several months. Tortures, rapes, murders — committed by an army that had fled the city and gone on to be slaughtered itself on the road to Baghdad. I wondered if bad things hung on to a place. If the evil that was almost palpable in the air was real or simply a creation of the dark and my own unease.[1]

Bad things do "hang on" to a place. Injustice opens the door for demonic oppression, an oppression that people are powerless to deal with outside of the cleansing, healing grace of God.

Filthy Nations Seeking Cleansing

As I write, Afghanistan is filled with warring factions; South Africa is marred by escalating black-on-black violence; Angola, Cambodia, Georgia and India are in anguish; and Germany is experiencing an ominous outpouring of venom against immigrants. The world is filthy in its unresolved guilt and desperate for cleansing. I have been surprised to see even secular politicians attempting reconciliation through open confession. Mikhail Gorbachev asked forgiveness, as a Russian, for the massacre of captive Polish officers during World War II. Polish leader, Lech Walesa, in turn asked forgiveness of the Jews in a historic speech before Israel's parliament, for Polish complicity with the Nazi slaughter of the Jews of the Warsaw ghetto and centuries of pogroms. The present Japanese government has formally apologized to the Koreans for Japan's harsh colonial rule of the Korean Peninsula from 1910 to 1945, and the trend will continue. However, acknowledgment is unleashing pent-up anger rather than bringing true healing.

The power of Jesus to enable forgiveness and reconciliation between peoples remains totally unique. Recently, a mature Christian boy, the only son of two lovely Christian parents and an almost fiancé to a young girl, was shot and killed at a video shop in Belfast, Northern Ireland, just so some terrorists could make the point that they were in town. One of my friends, attending Sunday service with the boy's parents, reported, "Their forgiveness, faith and love blew me away." This grace runs totally contrary to business as usual for the human heart.

What, then, is America's story? Where are the illegitimate gates that have given place to the enemy in our land? We live in an atmosphere heavy with spiritual oppression. God's face seems turned away from us. Idolatry and injustice are increasing within the land, and we have just experienced the greatest civil unrest in 130 years. Can we learn from our forefathers? Is there hope? Let's go to the Bible for answers. We can learn a lot from the story of Saul, David and the Gibeonites.

■ ■ ■

Note

1.   Kim Murphy, "On to Kuwait, Past the Saudis and the Censors," *Los Angeles Times,* March 5, 1991.

5

AN EXAMPLE
OF TERROR

It Happened Here

"The Lord will cause you to be defeated before your enemies; you shall go out one way against them, but you shall flee seven ways before them, and you shall be an example of terror to all the kingdoms of the earth."

Deuteronomy 28:25

To intrude on the battlefield at Gettysburg is to run a trembling hand over the most fevered scars on the American body. To stand on the river bluffs above Richmond is to gaze into another valley of sorrows. It was here that thousands of groaning, mutilated men came to die, swamping the crude field hospitals of a besieged city.

Just a few hundred yards away, Patrick Henry once shouted to another generation, "Give me liberty or give me death!" How could these killing fields claim descent from such a hopeful revolution? To what degree was the Civil War part of God's just judgment? Can we interpret the American story in the same way that the Bible exposes God's dealings with Israel?

Saul, David and the Gibeonites

David was finally victorious. The predictions of Samuel were
vindicated. Israel had a new king, but something was desperately wrong. The Bible records in 2 Samuel 21:1 that the land
was wasted by famine for three years. The cause was a mysterious drought. David inquired of the Lord the reason for this
calamity and learned that it was the bloodguiltiness of Saul, the
previous king.

Many generations previously, Joshua and the elders of
Israel had entered into a covenantal alliance with a people
named the Gibeonites, and Saul had violated it. Even though the
agreement was made without divine sanction, it was binding
because it was made in the name of the Lord, and a covenant is
a covenant. Saul broke this solemn covenant by slaughtering
the Gibeonites. This was a misguided attempt to win God's
favor through "ethnic cleansing," an action that violated God's
command not to pervert the justice due the alien living among
them (see Deut. 27:19).

"David said to the Gibeonites, 'What should I do for you?
And how can I make atonement that you may bless the inheritance of the Lord?'" (2 Sam. 21:3). In response, the Gibeonites
said, "'Let seven men of his descendants be delivered to us, and
we will hang them before the Lord in Gibeah of Saul, whom
the Lord chose'" (2 Sam. 21:6, *NKJV*).

David agreed, and the two sons of Rizpah, and the five
sons of Saul's daughter, Merab, were put to death and their
bodies left hanging on a rocky hill. Rizpah guarded their bodies
from carrion birds and beasts of prey until the October rains
began to fall, showing that God had accepted expiation for the
innocent blood that had polluted the land.

This is one of the most heartbreaking stories in the Bible.
It raises deeply disturbing questions about God's character.
Why did He apparently bless such an action? Why did this

cruel act restore His needed favor to the land?

Remember, sin can be atoned for in two ways. One would be literal payment, blood for blood—an exact balancing of the scales of justice. Or the application of the blood of the sacrifice. For years I have been asking Bible teachers to explain why David did not call upon the priests to make atonement for the land in the customary way. I have never received a satisfactory answer.*

The greatest grief must have been in the heart of God. He had created a path to cleansing, which would ultimately be centered on the blood of Jesus, but this provision was never applied in the case of the Gibeonites

Slavery in the Promised Land

This obscure story of the Gibeonites from the Bible could be closer to home than we think. The great sin of America has been to sacrifice all to wealth and empowerment. And the greatest expression of that sin was the institution of slavery, a system that persisted in this land long after it had been outlawed in most other places. Even at the time of the Revolution, the prophetic voice of the Methodist circuit rider was lifted in loud warning that God would bring great judgment if slavery was condoned.

John Wesley considered American slavery "the vilest that ever saw the sun."[1] Wesley's young disciple, Bishop Thomas Coke, went about the colonies preaching vociferously against slavery, to the approval of some and the outrage of others.

Preaching in Virginia in 1785, soon after the formation of the Methodist/Episcopal Church, the bishop urged every

---

*It could be that rampant murder committed by a privileged king was so abhorrent to God that it was not to be atoned for by sacrifice. This happened to the house of Eli, a generation before, because of the abuse of the sacrifice (see 1 Sam. 3:14).

preacher to circulate a petition to the General Assembly of that state, demanding that it make the emancipation of slaves legal. He, along with Bishop Asbury, even made a bold call upon George Washington, entreating him as a distinguished Virginian, to sign the petition and lend his influence to the cause. (Washington declined to sign, but assured the Methodists that he shared their sentiments and he would support the measure if it ever came to a hearing.)

Typical of the best of the circuit riders was Freeborn Garrettson of Maryland. He had entered the ministry at the age of 23, renouncing the world and obeying the edicts of a stringent conscience. Son of a prosperous planter, he inherited slaves, and after his conversion he stood in the midst of his household at family prayer and declared the slaves to be free. Nor was his conscience limited to the ethics of slavery. He was opposed to war, not being able to justify armed revolution as biblical. He refused military service, and he refused to take the oaths of loyalty when they were demanded of him by the states in which he traveled. He was often stoned, beaten with clubs and jailed, yet from 1775 on, Freeborn continued to preach without interruptions, except those imposed by jailers.

Compromise with the Devil

At the General Conference of 1784, the preachers voiced their determination "to extirpate this abomination from among us."[2] They decided that all Methodists must free their slaves within 12 months. They meant business, but they underestimated opposition from southern members living in states that had laws forbidding emancipation. This rule was suspended 5 months after it was made and eventually a compromise ruling permitted the holding of slaves but not "the buying and selling of men, women and children, with an intention to enslave them."[3] In other words, you could be a beneficiary of the slave trade but you were not to be a trader.

This trend to hypocritical compromise was to plague the American church and blunt its prophetic mandate. Indeed, by the 1840s, the compromised ministry began to lead the way toward confrontation and schism in the land. Questions arising out of the control of slavery led to a division of the Methodist/Episcopal church into northern and southern branches fully 16 years before the formation of the Confederate States of America. This division persisted for almost 100 years because of deep bitterness over the grievous effects of the Civil War and its aftermath.

The prophetic authority of the revived church first flared brightly in the postrevolution South, but then flickered out and was extinguished. Worse than that, the office of the prophet, exhorter and Bible teacher became bent, and many preachers began to distort Scripture to justify slavery as somehow part of God's natural order.* The shrill, self-righteous denunciation of some northern intellectuals and churchmen only deepened the divide. The Church had lost its sight. Truth was not declared, repentance did not come, the land was not cleansed and, like Saul of old, the leadership of the 1830s and 1840s were to cleanse the land with the blood of their children.

There was one last ray of hope. In 1857 and 1858, both north and south were mercifully visited with revival. If it had continued, history would no doubt be different, but the public

---

*Genesis 9:25 was a favorite text of many southern preachers. The black man was the subject of the "Hamitic curse" they said.

They failed to see that the passage simply prophesied that the depravity of Ham would manifest in Canaan and his descendants. The other three sons of Ham—Cush, Mizraim and Put—were not cursed. A study of the descendants of Ham reveals that the Babylonians, through Nimrod, are descendants of Cush and that Ham's descendants populated Palestine, Egypt and Ethiopia.

The prophecy finds its most likely fulfillment at the time of Joshua. The resident Canaanites were not black, whatever the interpretation; it had nothing to do with skin color.

mind became completely diverted by the turmoil and consternation caused by John Brown's raid and the political excitement of a grim campaign for the presidency. Although the fires of revival did not flicker out completely, the nation began to descend into an abyss.

How could the Church have failed so badly? Especially after great awakenings had united the land? After Wesley, Coke and others had sounded clear warning as far back as the 1770s?

Atoning with Our Blood

In spite of the surge of religious conversions occurring in some of the Confederate and Union camps, the awful slaughter began to unfold. Men could hear the singing of sacred hymns around the campfires of the enemy in the evening. Melodies of praise and devotion known to most Americans could be heard—and then the gray dawn would come. Terrified boys, praying to the same God, hurled themselves at each other. The carnage was unprecedented. The tactics of an older cavalier age met the ruthless realities of the weapons of the industrial era; 600,000 men were to die—2 percent of the national population—most of them Protestant believers after some fashion.

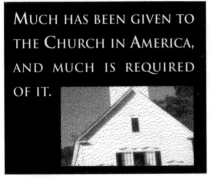

MUCH HAS BEEN GIVEN TO THE CHURCH IN AMERICA, AND MUCH IS REQUIRED OF IT.

The failure of the Church was its harsh denominational infighting over matters of doctrine. Methodists, Baptists, Presbyterians, Disciples of Christ and Universalists kept elevating the rhetoric of self-righteous denunciation of one another. The harshest words were reserved for the debate over slavery. More often than not, even Abolitionists, proclaiming the truth, did so in such an un-Christlike manner that reconciliation with their views became almost impossible for their opponents.

As the Los Angeles Police Department (LAPD) did during the riots of 1992, the Church had lost the moral authority necessary to protect the land. The LAPD was supposed to protect the citizenry, but the actions of some of its own members had provided the match to the tinder, and the police waited in uncertainty behind their barricades. So it was with the Church of the 1860s. The salt that had lost its flavor was, literally, trampled underfoot. Much had been given to the Church in America, and much was required of it.

Man of Destiny

It was not a preacher, but a rough-hewn frontier politician who finally seemed to grasp what was happening to the nation. The words of Abraham Lincoln instruct us still. He called Americans the "almost chosen people."[4] What thinking lies behind those words?

Abraham Lincoln was a man of unconventional faith who regularly attended Presbyterian churches in Springfield and Washington, pastored by doctrinal conservatives. Yet he never became a member of any congregation, having little time for Christian creeds or statements of faith.

An immense separation exists between pre-Civil War America's puritan-based culture and the narcissism of today. The common people were not preoccupied with theological complexities; they feared God and lived out a simple wisdom rooted in common sense and experience. Lincoln was a man of the common people, a God-fearing, humorous, earthy pragmatist.

As president, Lincoln was initially committed to the Union

above all else. This was his idol; it was his own version of nationalism that drove him. He vacillated on the slavery question. He disapproved of it, but was in no hurry. It was not until July 1862, well into the Civil War, that the president summoned his cabinet and laid before it for discussion an Emancipation Proclamation. There was agreement in principle, but it was feared that emancipation would only be seen as a political manipulation to gain the favor of Britain and France, and thus an admission of weakness. The Union had experienced a series of military disasters and Secretary Seward was afraid that the Proclamation would be seen as "the last shriek of our retreat."[5] Lincoln concurred.

Unlike most presidents, Lincoln functioned literally as the commander in chief, personally mapping strategy. Despite victories, such as the capture of Fort Donelson in Tennessee by Grant and the occupation of New Orleans by Farragut, the north was being bled in battle after battle. Thirteen thousand Union troops became casualties at Shiloh and the battles at Bull Run and Harper's Ferry were crushing defeats. Lee fought McClellan at Antietam and had huge losses on both sides and an inconclusive result.

Five days after the battle Lincoln finally issued a preliminary Emancipation Proclamation, but it was not until three months later that the final version was published. "Things had gone from bad to worse," he confessed later, "until I felt that we had reached the end of our rope on the plan of operations we had been pursuing; that we had about played our last card, and must change our tactics or lose the game."[6]

Here was a desperate man, playing with moral absolutes for political expediency. "An act of justice" as well as "a fit and necessary war measure," said Lincoln.[7] It was a half measure. It freed slaves only in those areas of the Confederacy still in rebellion, not in loyal slave states or areas under Union occupation.

Seward admonished, "We show our sympathy by emancipating the slaves where we cannot reach them and holding them in bondage where we can set them free."[8] Apparently he was not the only one who was unimpressed by Lincoln's actions. The God of nations was not prepared to compromise the Day of Judgment and the inconclusive slaughter continued.

The president, in his frustration, changed generals as often as he changed his shirts. Burnside succeeded McClellan, and after Lee's victory at Fredricksburg, Hooker replaced Burnside, who was in turn replaced by Meade. Chancellorsville saw a crushing defeat of Union forces and then came the greatest and most decisive battle of the War: Gettysburg.

Northern victory was far from inevitable, for the South was not fighting a war of conquest (unwinnable, given their inferiority in man power and wealth), but a struggle to induce war weariness and to compel the North to recognize their boundaries. The Confederacy had almost succeeded in 1863. Its armies were deep into Pennsylvania. Draft riots were about to break out in New York City. The first regiment of black volunteers had been armed — not because of a sense of racial justice, but because of an urgent need for more men. This is the context of Gettysburg, July 1-3, 1863.

Robert E. Lee made a fateful error in thinking that his guns had knocked out the Union battery, and he sent his men into the nightmare of Pickett's charge.

Suppose we could rerun history and give Lee another chance. This time, armed with better intelligence perhaps, he does not blunder and prevails. In this replay, the South might win the war and all subsequent American history would be radically changed. Was it really coincidence, or generalship? Were the Union generals really so inept and the Confederates, Lee, Jackson and Stewart, so brilliant? Why was that brilliance suddenly replaced by stumbling misfortune? What really happened that made Gettysburg so different? It was not a complete Union victory, but it was the beginning of the end for Lee because it was so costly. Perhaps God was giving Lincoln some encouragement, forging understanding in his tormented mind.

Let Justice Roll Down

To most of the people of the day, the war was about the rights of states and the degree to which central government should be empowered. But to the living God, the bitter cup of slavery was full, and justice could no longer be delayed. God was not only committed to the slaves, but also to the generations of Americans yet unborn.

Why should future Americans be born into a land polluted with injustice from which God's glory had departed? Why should they endure a demonized atmosphere, endlessly reaping contention because their ancestors had broken covenant with God by turning a land of refuge into a defiant stronghold of enslavement? God saw that the Church had failed in its prophetic and priestly role, leaving no alternative but the cleansing of the land through releasing long-delayed judgment.

The Civil War continued inconclusively into 1864. Grant had a victory at Chattanooga and was named general in chief of the Union armies. However, in the wilderness (near Richmond) at Spotsylvania, and at Cold Harbor, his forces suffered more than 60,000 casualties. He then became involved in a 10-month siege of Petersburg, losing thousands of men to the deeply entrenched Confederates blocking Richmond's encirclement.

Against this backdrop, the thinking of the president and the Republican party began to change. On June 8, Lincoln was nominated for a second term. Both regular and rump Republican conventions affirmed support for a constitutional amendment to abolish all slavery forever. It was passed by the Senate in April 1864, having the president's full support. Lincoln's priorities had finally changed. They were now going forward "in the joint names of liberty (for slaves) and Union," Lincoln said.[9]

For the first time, steady reports of victory began to come from the front, most significantly the capture of Atlanta on September 1 by General Sherman. When Lincoln took the oath of office on March 4, 1865, he could look with satisfaction on a string of victories from Nashville to Savannah.

> LINCOLN UNDERSTOOD THAT WE ALL STAND GUILTY BEFORE GOD— EVEN THOSE CALLING FOR REPENTANCE.

In his second inaugural address, President Lincoln reveals his deep contemplation on God and the divine will. Here he proclaims his belief that the founding ideals of the nation made each generation stewards of a uniquely moral vision; that these ideals, grounded in the Scriptures, show us how far short we fall in most of our national life; and that God's judgment falls righteously upon us all, if we sanction or tolerate abuses against humanity. Most of all this speech revealed a profound respect for God's providential rule over the affairs of nations. Here is an excerpt:

> If we shall suppose that American slavery is one of those offenses, in which, in the providence of God, must needs come, but which, having continued through His appointed time, He now wills to remove, and that He gives to both North and South this terrible war, as the woe due to those by whom the offense came, shall we discern therein any departure from those Divine Attributes which the believers in a living God always ascribe to Him?
>
> Fondly do we hope—fervently do we pray—that this mighty scourge of war may speedily pass away. Yet, if God wills that it continue, until all the wealth

piled up by the bond-mans 250 years of unrequited toil shall be sunk, and every drop of blood drawn from the lash, shall be paid by another drawn with the sword, as was said 3000 years ago, so still must be said, "The judgments of the Lord are true and righteous altogether."[10]

Of the many people who have called the nation to repentance, few had the clear sight of Lincoln. He saw how thoroughly good and evil are intermingled in the national heritage; so many others have equated the United States with either transcendent good or more recently, with pervasive evil. Lincoln understood that we all stand guilty before God—even those calling for repentance.

One month after the president clarified these eternal issues in the speech quoted above, Lee surrendered to Grant at Appomattox Courthouse. The war that cost more lives than all the other struggles in United States history put together was finally over. Of all the peoples of the earth, it is Americans who have just cause to tremble before a righteous God, in the light of our experience of His just judgments. Our history reveals that God's hand is heavy upon us, and that in the final analysis we have never gotten away with a thing.

"The Lord reigns, let the peoples tremble" (Ps. 99:1).

■ ■ ■

Notes
1. Susanne Everett, *History of Slavery* (Secaucus, NJ: Chantwell Books, Inc., 1992), p. 134.
2. Charles W. Ferguson, "Organizing to Beat the Devil," *Methodists and the Making of America* (New York: Doubleday, 1983), p. 20.

3. Ibid., p. 21.
4. Mark A. Wall, "The Puzzling Faith of Abraham Lincoln," *Christian History* magazine, Issue 33, Vol. XI, No. 1.
5. *The American Heritage Book of the Presidents*, Vol. V. The editors of *American Heritage* magazine (New York: Dell Publishing, n.d.), p. 415.
6. Ibid.
7. Ibid., p. 416.
8. Ibid.
9. Ibid., p. 418.
10. Quotations taken from "The Works of Abraham Lincoln — State Papers," 1861-1865, Vol. VI, 1907.

6

ARE WE CURSED, OR WHAT?

If God Be for You...

"But it shall come about, if you will not obey the Lord your God, to observe to do all His commandments and His statutes with which I charge you today, that all these curses shall come upon you and overtake you."

Deuteronomy 28:15

In Deuteronomy 28, we read a list of disastrous things that will happen to a people under what is called, "the curse of God."

I began to write this book during the war with Iraq (the Gulf War), and was horrified to note that here in California we were experiencing many of the details on this list from Deuteronomy, including an unbroken drought, a falling economy and an exponential increase in incurable diseases. Worst of all, more than 400,000 young military personnel faced the boastful claims of Saddam Hussein's military machine. I was deeply troubled.

It was January the 15th, 1991. The United Nations deadline for Iraq's withdrawal from Kuwait was past. We were about

to be at war. Did Saddam have nuclear capability? What about
chemical weapons and missiles? The United States government
expected victory, yet had prepared 40,000 hospital beds, from
West Germany to California. A huge medical task force waited
to receive our maimed and dying young people.

Large gatherings of believers met to pray. We were very
aware of the times Israel had been defeated in this type of circumstance. Just because the enemy was more wicked than
Israel did not mean that God would not use them to chastise
His people.

You might say, "But isn't this text in Deuteronomy a spe-
cific prophecy, written to the Jews in ancient times?" Yes, it is,
but God's way of dealing with His people is a prophetic prototype for all nations in all generations. Through the experience of
the chosen people, every people group on earth was to receive
instruction of God's ways.

"But it is Old Testament. Hasn't all this changed since
Jesus shed His blood? Isn't this stuff about a curse all behind us
because of the Cross?" No. It is not until the glory of the New
Jerusalem is revealed that we read, "The leaves of the tree were
for the healing of the nations. And there shall be no more curse"
(NKJV). Notice the use of the future tense—and we find this in
Revelation 22:2,3, which is the last chapter in our Bibles.

Remember, we are talking about nations here, not an individual's salvation. Paul said in Romans 1:18: "For the wrath of
God is revealed from heaven against all ungodliness and
unrighteousness of men." These curses would be inevitable for
us personally, were it not for Jesus, who has "redeemed us from
the curse of the Law, having become a curse for us" (Gal. 3:13).

Recovering the Glory

"Then what *is* the curse of God?" First of all, Deuteronomy 28 is not referring to any kind of hex caused by demonic powers through the agency of a medium, although we sometimes use the same word. Second, it is not an angry Creator, losing control of Himself and doing nasty things. Deuteronomy 28 is not a warning about some weakness in God's character. This same heavenly Father was revealed in Jesus. Jesus' trials at Gethsemane and the cross contained greater temptations to vindictive behavior than any personality in the universe had ever endured, yet the self-control of Christ held. No wonder we can trust Him.

In one sense, the curse of God could be seen as the absence of God's needed favor. Many people understand that God is holy and that sin causes the withdrawal of His revealed presence, but we tend to think that things just keep on going as they are: The rain will fall, the crops will come in. Children will be born, life goes on. But is it true? Life does not go on. Life is not a factor, but a person. "And He is before all things, and in Him all things hold together" (Col. 1:17).

Jesus said, "I am the way, and the truth, and the life" (John 14:6). The words "way" and "truth" are easy to understand. But what did He mean when He said "life"? That's a biological term? We have a word for the absence of life: death. Look again at Deuteronomy 28. It's a litany of death. God's revealed presence is not an optional extra. The worst thing that could be written over your life, your church, your city or your nation is Ichabod—"The glory has departed" (1 Sam. 4:21).

It is not that God abdicates His governance of one square inch of this planet. His pursuing grace continues. "Where sin abounded, grace did much more abound" (Rom. 5:20, *KJV*). But His revealed presence is veiled. "Thou hast covered thyself with a cloud, that our prayer should not pass through" (Lam. 3:44, *KJV*).

Much more terrifying than the presence of the adversary is the curse that results when the Lord turns His face away from us. This is what happened to Israel at Ai because of Achan's sin. "Therefore the sons of Israel cannot stand before their enemies;...for they have become accursed. I will not be with you anymore" (Josh. 7:12).

Our prime objective, therefore, in intercession and spiritual warfare, is not the removal of the enemy, but the return of the glory. The restoration of God's needed favor. When we encounter a spiritual stronghold, it is not a testimony to the presence of a *big* demon, but rather to the absence of the glory of God. Just as nature abhors a vacuum, so it is in the unseen realm. When the glory departs, the demons rush in. We have an enemy that swarms to woundedness and corruption: Beelzebub, lord of the flies. His weapons are accusation and deception, his strongholds are the places of unresolved guilt and wounding within the land.

The Sins of Nations

Here is an improbable event: Thousands of people standing in a streambed, shouting, "I will not have sex with my mother-in-law!" It happened, and it was serious stuff. We find the occasion reported in Deuteronomy 27. From verse 15 on, every phrase begins with the words, "Cursed is he." The Levites proclaimed these 12 statements when the people crossed Jordan into the Promised Land, and the people shouted agreement with a loud, "Amen."

Every intercessor should know Deuteronomy 27, because it lists the conditions under which God's glory will depart from a land. It is, therefore, a foundational text for those who want to see the healing of America's wounds, and the breaking of satanic strongholds. At first reading, these statements may strike you as bizarre. They appear to be a strange assortment of sins, randomly presented. It is only when we meditate upon the foundational premise behind each phrase that we begin to see why these particular word pictures were chosen to express a nation's agreement with God. Let's take a look at the list.

Idolatry

The sin of idolatry is the first subject addressed in this very public covenant.

> 1. Consider verse 15: "Cursed is the man who makes an idol or a molten image, an abomination to the Lord, the work of the hands of the craftsman, and sets it up in secret."

Although most Americans do not bow to carved images, idolatry is everywhere. It is idolatry to look to human institutions for protection, provision and direction instead of to the Father. It is idolatry to look to human saviors for deliverance, instead of to Jesus, the Son. It is idolatry to look to false religion and vain philosophies for understanding, instead of to the Holy Spirit, who alone brings revelation knowledge. Anything that counterfeits the work and place of the Trinity is idolatry. It's not that God has a need for our attention or allegiance, it's just that He loves us. He knows that the hopes of mankind are false hopes if not focused on Him.

All sin is a violation of some type of relationship. Idolatry is a sin against God Himself, but it always carries a by-product called injustice. Everything God does and says promotes convergence, harmony and intimacy. Every device of Satan is aimed at breaking relationships, producing alienation and isolation. Evil at its deepest root is the self-sufficient pride that refuses intimacy in favor of control.

Note that the next 11 Scripture verses all mention people wounding people. Each verse illustrates a type of injustice.

Injustice

2. Verse 16: "Cursed is he who dishonors his father or mother."
Failing to give honor to those who deserve it. Refusing to acknowledge your debt to those who have gone before.

Remember this is about a nation. In our case, we can't deal with the dark side of American history until we acknowledge our debt to the Anglo-Saxon Protestants for laying a foundation for the unique attributes of the United States. Their contribution created the distinctives that draw immigrants to this land to this day. In the 1960s, there was a tendency to revise history, to teach it in a way that vilified and mocked the pilgrims and the founding fathers. This was a lie, equal to the earlier tendency to sanctify all their actions. Both extremes displease God because they fall short of the truth. A strong Christian heritage movement has emerged since 1976 that seeks to give proper honor to righteous ancestors, particularly through Christian schools. This will be helpful as long as we search out the whole truth as God would see it.

3. Verse 17: "Cursed is he who moves his neighbor's boundary mark."
To violate that which is a matter of solemn covenant.

Our treatment of Native Americans comes to mind. More than 300 treaties were violated. We will deal with this in great detail in chapter 11.

4. Verse 18: "Cursed is he who misleads a blind person on the road."
Showing cruelty to the helpless, failure to teach the proper path.

The question here is, how do we handle our power, particularly the power that comes with knowledge? Superior knowledge can be used to serve the weak or exploit them.

An example could be the practices of management in agrobusiness and industry, which have often fallen short of God's standards. We have a long history of grievance, confrontation and violence within the American marketplace. And, today, we have continuing tension, particularly surrounding the practice of exploiting cheap labor in offshore plants in poorer nations. Applying ethics to business is far from simple. There *are* Bible-based solutions, but they have seldom been applied.

> 5. Verse 19: "Cursed is he who distorts the justice due an alien, orphan, and widow."
> *The exploitation of minority races or those who are disadvantaged and weak by virtue of family tragedy.*

Among other things, this is a clear indictment of the enslavement of Africans in the New World. From the indentured labor of the 1600s to the abusive handling of Chinese labor in California and the West, America's story has been marked by the abuse of justice in governing the powerless.

> 6. Verse 20: "Cursed is he who lies with his father's wife, because he has uncovered his father's skirt."
> *Destroying the integrity of your father's family. Coveting more than your rightful inheritance.*

This and the next three declarations deal with sexual sin and the violation of the family. The family is the basic building block of nationhood, consisting of a circle of covenantal love and romantic attraction, into which a tiny dependent creature is born, and then loved unconditionally. The family as a unit, when indwelt by the Holy Spirit, represents the Trinitarian nature of our loving God in a way that cannot be equaled by an individual man or woman of God, no matter how devout. For this reason, family integrity must be retained.

At one time, I found myself giving counsel to three separate women who were involved in lesbian relationships but wanted to follow Christ. I asked each one the same question. "You know the Bible condemns homosexual relationships, why do you think God does this?" Each person gave the same answer. "Same-sex marriage produces no children, and God commands us to be fruitful and multiply, so I guess that's why God disapproves." I pointed out that this answer falls dangerously short of God's true intent. Children need both Mom and Dad. To distort God's order for the family is to tamper with the earth's most foundational picture of God's own nature, character and personality. It's like altering the DNA in a multiplying cell and causing mutation. Eventually a nation becomes a reflection of the weaknesses or strengths of its families.

7. Verse 21: "Cursed is he who lies with any animal."
Failure to maintain the unique dignity of humankind, we are flesh, but made in the image of God.

8. Verse 22: "Cursed is he who lies with his sister, the daughter of his father or of his mother."
Using family intimacy for fraudulent gratification. Usurping the privileges belonging to others. Despoiling the gifts your family has to give to others. Using your gender strengths destructively.

Incest that is initiated by male relatives has only recently been revealed as a huge national problem that leaves millions of American women scarred for life. But there is more to this when we look at incest as a concept. I believe a denomination can incestuously use its gifts to bless only those within its family boundaries instead of blessing and serving the whole kingdom of God. This is equally true of nations. When the United States poured its resources into a shattered Europe after World War II, it distanced itself from this sin. The Marshall Plan is one cause for the favor of God upon this nation; more about that later.

9. Verse 23: "Cursed is he who lies with his mother-in-law."
Destroying the integrity of your wife's family, rejecting the boundaries that love dictates, lawlessness.

This is rebellion taken to the extreme. We have become a nation famous for accepting no limits on personal behavior. We not only practice deviance, but we also film it and sell it to the world.

10. Verse 24: "Cursed is he who strikes his neighbor in secret."
Covetous and deceitful competition.

In our day, this is most evident in business practice, particularly in sales and marketing. Some industries, such as real estate development, are notorious for seducing people with inflated claims of value and then leaving them with broken promises and heavy debt.

11. Verse 25: "Cursed is he who accepts a bribe to strike down an innocent person."
Using a position of authority to pervert justice.

12. Verse 26: "Cursed is he who does not confirm the words of this law by doing them."
To devalue sacred truths through a life of hypocrisy.

Now think of the America of the 1990s. What is there in our current conduct that violates God's loving standards? Where do the strongholds exist in our land? When and where did the glory depart? How do we reclaim it?

Don't just think about contemporary values and the sins of individuals. There are many parts to American society. For example, when we look at our short history we see ample reason for God's continuing judgment. So much has never been made right.

We *must* put the past behind us, but we must do it in a biblical way. Have we done that? Wounds that stand open and uncleansed do not heal with the passage of time. Worst of all, God has never lowered His standards for any generation or any nation. If His face is turned from us, there will be no healing in the land.

The Meek Shall Inherit

Remember, our objective in spiritual warfare is to come into right relationship with God in order to see His face turned back toward us. We face an adversary in this brief, terrestrial apprenticeship, but everything really comes back to our relationship with God. Who kept Moses and his generation out of the Promised Land? Canaanite armies? The territorial spirits long entrenched by Canaanite idolatry? No. It was God.

We need to be in right order with one another. We need to be in right standing before God. "He who overcomes shall inherit these things," says Revelation 21:7. That's what it's all about; through fighting the good fight we displace the enemy and qualify to inherit God's promises for our land. "'And I will not hide My face from them any longer, for I shall have poured out My Spirit on the house of Israel,' declares the Lord God" (Ezek. 39:29).

We have been given weapons that are "mighty in God for pulling down strongholds" (2 Cor. 10:4, *NKJV*), but they are strange weapons. Among them: repentance, confession, forgiveness, reconciliation and restitution.

It is no surprise to me that the war in the Middle East was not a disaster for America. Not because of F11-7A Stealth fighter bombers, or six aircraft carrier groups, but because I witnessed such repentance in the months prior to the war.

My book *Taking Our Cities for God* had been published a few months before, and I was traveling from city to city, ministering at citywide pastors' gatherings. In more than 20 years of travel throughout the United States, I had never seen the depth of repentance and tears that I saw during that time. In city after city, weeping would sweep across the auditorium and then people would stand up and pour out their hearts in confession, completely identifying with our national sins.

I remember one pastors' gathering in particular. It was in the harbor district of Los Angeles, a place where division was more common than unity. It was Tuesday morning in drought-stricken California.

As I drove toward the gathering, the rain began to pour down. The radio broadcast news of the war. A sweeping victory was unfolding in the first hours of the ground war. General Schwartzkopf later called it a "miracle." Review of statistics indicated that it was safer on that battlefield for an American soldier than in the troubled parts of our own cities. Amazing, when we consider that millions of dollars of ordinance was exploding in all directions across that battlefield.

Inside the church, there was no elation among the gathered pastors. War is terrible. It always indicates some degree of failure for the international Church. I still remember the prayer of one pastor. "Oh Lord, we are all here in unity at last. The rain is pouring down and our children are not dying in this war." Then he began to weep. We all wept. Relief, mingled with holy fear.

We knew that we still stood in a land deserving judgment and that God indeed will judge.

> For thus says the Lord of hosts,
> "Cut down her trees, and cast up a siege against
> Jerusalem.
> This is the city to be punished,
> In whose midst there is only oppression.
> As a well keeps its waters fresh,
> So she keeps fresh her wickedness.
> Violence and destruction are heard in her;
> Sickness and wounds are ever before Me.
> Be warned, O Jerusalem,
> Lest I be alienated from you;
> Lest I make you a desolation,
> A land not inhabited" (Jer. 6:6-8).

That day no one could see the great calamity looming over our future. Not on a distant battlefield, but in the heart of America. That afternoon I drove back to my neighborhood, passing the corner just two blocks away that most people in the world were about to see. The place of the beating of Rodney King.

What Do You Think?

In this chapter I have suggested a foundational premise for each of the covenantal statements made by Israel as they entered the Promised Land, as recorded in Deuteronomy 27. Meditate on these 12 verses and to come up with your own thoughts about what they mean and how they apply to America.

■ ■ ■

PART II

BROKEN WALLS, FESTERING WOUNDS

*"And they have healed the brokenness of
My people superficially, saying 'Peace, Peace,'
but there is no peace."*

Jeremiah 6:14

7

I FEEL LIKE
CRYING NOW

Identification with
the Sins of the Nation

*"Hear the prayer of Your servant which I pray before
You now, day and night, for the children of Israel Your
servants, and confess the sins of the children of Israel
which we have sinned against You. Both my father's house
and I have sinned."*

Nehemiah 1:6 (*NKJV*)

What was true in Nehemiah's day is true today. A repentant
church, confessing the sins of the nation before God, is America's only hope. As we have seen, Abraham Lincoln recognized
this truth. During the darkest days of the Civil War, he summoned the people to:

> "Recognize the hand of God in this terrible visitation," and to "sorrowful remembrance of our own
> faults and crimes as a nation and as individuals, to
> humble ourselves before Him and to pray for His
> mercy—to pray that we may be spared further punishment, though most justly deserved."[1]

President Lincoln gave warning in his proclamation of March 30, 1863:

> It is the duty of nations as well as of men, to own their dependence upon the overruling power of God; to confess their sins and transgressions in humble sorrow, yet with assured hope that genuine repentance will lead to mercy and pardon.[2]

This was a proclamation to all citizens. To the pagan it says, "Repent!" and to the Christian also, but the unredeemed cannot make atonement for the land. The pagan cannot go up into the gap and present the blood of the Lamb. This is the privilege and responsibility of God's people; even if they are just a remnant in the land.

The judgment of God is as real today as it was in ancient Egypt when the plagues came. Remember when the death angel took the firstborn of man and beast during the last plague? The Jews were not delivered because they were morally superior. Their salvation depended on the sacrifice of a perfect lamb. "Moreover, they shall take some of the blood and put it on the two doorposts and on the lintel of the houses" (Exod. 12:7).

Unknowingly, many Jewish fathers made the sign of the cross as they placed the blood overhead and side to side. God was laying foundations for our human understanding of the atonement. "'The blood shall be a sign for you on the houses where you live; and when I see the blood I will pass over you, and no plague will befall you to destroy you when I strike the land of Egypt'" (Exod. 12:13).

Through the Temple ceremonies, generations of Israelite priests made atonement for the land in this way as they looked forward to the Messiah. We do the same thing, as we present the blood, looking back 2,000 years to the Cross. But imagine this. What if one Jewish father decided not to put the blood on the doorpost? That family would have received the full consequence of the plague, awaking next morning to a dead child. Christian Americans are in the position of that father. There *is* a perfect lamb, the blood *has* been shed, *but the blood must be applied.*

The Missing Key

The question is: What is the role of the Church in presenting the blood? How do we do that? How do we restore God's needed favor and bring healing to the land? We have the promise, but what is the process?

In 1976, 2 Chronicles 7:14 was written like a banner over America. Prominent songwriters, Jimmy and Carol Owens, turned it into a popular Scripture chorus, and the theme of large worship and prayer gatherings. Today's prayer movements had their beginnings at that time, and it seems that every organization quoted this Scripture in its brochure, letterhead or statement of purpose. Eventually, half a million people gathered during "Washington for Jesus," the hope of its promise as the dominant theme.

"[If] My people, who are called by My name will humble themselves and pray, and seek My face and turn from their wicked ways, then I will hear from heaven, will forgive their sin, and will heal their land" (2 Chron. 7:14).

It's time to examine this passage again. Particularly the question, What does it really mean for God's people to *humble themselves?* First, let's look at the context.

David has died, and Solomon has inherited the task of building the Temple. The work has finally been completed, and Solomon has an awesome experience, a personal visit from God. "Then the Lord appeared to Solomon at night and said to him, 'I have heard your prayer and have chosen this place for Myself as a house of sacrifice'" (2 Chron. 7:12). Here God explains the purpose of the Temple. It is to be the place where the blood is presented for the purpose of removing guilt. As New Testament Scripture says, "Without shedding of blood there is no remission [of sins]" (Heb. 9:22, *NKJV*).

Then God briefly refers to the curses in Deuteronomy 28. "If I shut up the heavens so that there is no rain, or if I command the locust to devour the land, or if I send pestilence among My people" (2 Chron. 7:13).

Then the conditions of heart and attitude God needed to see are mentioned. It's obvious that a ritualistic presentation of the blood by an unrepentant people would *not* make atonement for the land. God was looking for genuine responses on the part of His people before the land would be healed.

Let's look at these conditions.

"[If] My people who are called by My name." He's addressing us, not the pagans. America will be cursed or blessed according to the obedience or disobedience of the Church.

"Will humble themselves." This is the statement we understand least and neglect the most. We understand what it means to pray and to repent, but what does it really mean for us to humble ourselves?

As an exercise, go ahead and feel immensely humble right now. See if you can do it. It doesn't really work, does it? Humility has to be more than a pious mood. It is an attitude expressed through dynamic action. The most obvious action associated with humility is thanksgiving; to acknowledge our debt to another. When God sees a grateful heart, he reads humility, but there is a far more radical action, an action that brings both cleansing and healing. The act of confession.

"If we confess our sins, He is faithful and righteous to forgive us our sins and to cleanse us from all unrighteousness" (1 John 1:9).

"Confess your faults one to another,...that you may be healed" (Jas. 5:16).

The act of confession is as powerful in effecting the cleansing and healing of nations as it is in individuals.

In many ways, America has become worse since 1976, particularly the alienation between genders, races and political ideologies. At "Washington for Jesus," a huge gathering on the mall, we briefly made mention of our national sins, but was it enough? Have we ever really practiced in America the identificational repentance exemplified by the priests and prophets of the Bible?

> OUR GOD IS A GOD OF PATIENCE AND COMPASSION BEYOND HUMAN COMPREHENSION.

Is it possible that evangelical Christians have devalued confession because of our roots? There was great abuse of the confessional prior to the Reformation. Are we in a state of reaction? What is really biblical? What is the posture of the interceding Church in the midst of a land polluted with blood and blinded by self-sufficiency?

Stark Honesty

I was once visited by a businessman who had been listening to my teachings by cassette tape. "I don't know how you can have such hope," he said. "This culture is rotten to the core."

How would you answer him? It's true, wickedness is woven into the fabric of our culture. Is there hope?

The gospel reveals a message of faith, hope and love. *Faith* is receiving the knowledge of the Father's ability and character; *hope* is the expectation of His goodness to me; *love* is the experience of intimate affection, the embrace of the Father, His grace poured out. But the promise of the gospel is only realized as human hearts identify with Christ, our great intercessor, in His ongoing labor of prayer. That is why the intercessor weeps. Like Jesus, he or she identifies with both God and man.

The great intercessors of the Bible all approached God with a genuine sense of shame and embarrassment. They did not come into God's presence in order to cover up sin, but to agree with His assessment of it, to face with stark honesty the wickedness of the culture around them.

"For they proceed from evil to evil,
And they do not know Me," says the Lord.
"Everyone take heed to his neighbor,
And do not trust any brother;
For every brother will utterly supplant,
And every neighbor will walk with slanderers.
Everyone will deceive his neighbor,
And will not speak the truth;
They have taught their tongue to speak lies,
And weary themselves to commit iniquity"
(Jer. 9:3-5, NKJV).

Intercession is not an escape from reality. Our communication with God must be rooted in the truth—the eternal truth of His holy standards and the awful truth about American society as God sees it. The intercessor experiences the broken heart of God through the indwelling presence of the Holy Spirit. The intercessor also identifies with the sin of the people, because the intercessor has personally contributed to God's grief.

Our God is a God of patience and compassion beyond human comprehension. His torment is poured out through the prophecy of Jeremiah.

"Why have they provoked Me to anger
With their carved images,

And with foreign idols?...
For the hurt of the daughter of my people I am hurt.
I am mourning;...
Oh, that my head were waters,
And my eyes a fountain of tears,
That I might weep day and night
For the slain of the daughter of my people!"
(Jer. 8:19,21; 9:1, *NKJV*).

In responding to the broken heart of God, we need to identify with the sins of the nation in personal and corporate repentance. When Nehemiah prayed for the restoration of Israel, he did not pray for the nation as if he were not part of it. He said, "I and my father's people have sinned" (Neh 1:6).

Ezra went even further when he said, "Oh my God: I am too ashamed and humiliated to lift up my face to You, my God; for our iniquities have risen higher than our heads, and our guilt has grown up to the heavens" (Ezra 9:6, *NKJV*).

My Sin, Our Sin

Both Nehemiah and Ezra were righteous men. You may be a righteous person who is not involved in any direct way with the vices present in this nation. But no temptation is not common to humanity (see 1 Cor. 10:13). We can all identify with the roots of any given sin. "For all have sinned and fall short of the glory of God" (Rom. 3:23).

Take, for example, the shedding of innocent blood in the act of abortion. You may never have participated in an abortion, but all of us have been guilty of the root sins that give place to such an activity. I can think of five common roots that lead to abortion: lust, the love of comfort, the love of money, rejection and unbelief.

- *Lust,* because it is often the context for irresponsible conception.
- *The love of comfort,* because the decision to abort is often made simply to avoid the discomfort of pregnancy.
- *The love of money,* because of a choice to avoid financial sacrifice even though a human life is at stake.
- *Rejection,* because in her fear of rejection by society or boyfriend, a woman's solution is to in fact reject the child in her womb.
- *Unbelief,* because we discount the existence of a just God who will surely honor a difficult but righteous decision. The voice of unbelief concludes, "If I have this baby, it will ruin my whole life!"

These are struggles common to us all and illustrate, therefore, the need for honest identification with the sins of our nation when we "stand in the gap" (Ezek. 22:30) asking for God's mercy. Nehemiah and the families with him assembled themselves before the Lord with fasting, in sackcloth and with dust on their heads. Though they were just a remnant, they completely identified with their nation and its history. "Then those of Israelite lineage separated themselves from all foreigners; and they stood and confessed their sins and the iniquities of their fathers" (Neh. 9:2, *NKJV*).

When we ask for God's mercy on others, we should never say, "How could they do such a thing?" We know exactly how they could do it, because the potential for the worst evil lies within each one of us, apart from God's saving grace and the life of Christ within us. Paul said, "I find then the principle that evil is present in me, the one who wishes to do good" (Rom. 7:21).

God often gives me an objective in prayer and fills me with faith for an answer. I may be praying for a needy neighbor or praying for the nation. As I struggle in prayer for others to be released from spiritual bondage, the Lord begins to reveal the depravity of my own heart.

The issues here are humility and honesty. God cannot use an unclean vessel in the place of intercession. "If I regard iniquity in my heart, the Lord will not hear" (Ps. 66:18, *NKJV*). First cleansing, then power. "Sanctify yourselves, for tomorrow the Lord will do wonders among you" (Josh. 3:5, *NKJV*).

> THE HOLY SPIRIT PRAYS THROUGH US AS THE DIVINE INTERCESSOR, BUT LIMITS HIMSELF TO EXERCISING AN AUTHORITY PROPORTIONATE TO THE YIELDEDNESS OF THE HUMAN VESSEL.

We need to gain a place where not only do we trust God, but God also trusts us. "Search me, O God, and know my heart; try me and know my anxieties; and see if there is any wicked way in me, and lead me in the way everlasting" (Ps. 139:23,24, *NKJV*).

When God has tested us and found a heart totally dedicated to His purpose, then He gives the promise of access to His power. "If you abide in Me, and My words abide in you, you will ask what you desire, and it shall be done for you" (John 15:7, *NKJV*). At this point, our prayers become effective in releasing power that changes things. "Confess your trespasses to one another, and pray for one another, that you may be healed. The effective, fervent prayer of a righteous man avails much" (Jas. 5:16, *NKJV*).

The Holy Spirit prays through us as the divine intercessor "with groanings which cannot be uttered" (Rom. 8:26, *NKJV*), but limits Himself to exercising an authority proportionate to the yieldedness of the human vessel.

It is my own testimony that the victories of my life have always come in the midst of repentance and confession.

When I come back to the Cross, I experience again cleansing and forgiveness. The consequences of my sin have fallen upon the Lamb that was slain. The blood is again sprinkled on the doorposts of my heart. Instead of perfecting righteousness in me, He who *is* righteous is standing up within me and beginning to live His life. Jesus is the only person who can truly live the Christian life. I must acknowledge again my total dependence on Him.

We are by nature incomplete. Human beings by definition are the dwelling place of God. God has created us as a vessel for His own being. In a sense, we cannot be fully human apart from Him.

Jesus doesn't dispense His attributes to us as we need them. He doesn't give us *some* love. He *is* love. His life unleashed within us is the source of all victory and blessing. He is everything that I am not. He is consistently loving, completely honest and quick to forgive. My only hope is to consciously acknowledge my desperate need of Him. "Jesus, live Your life through me," has become my daily prayer.

My biggest problem is not demons. I am my biggest problem. It is only when God has cleansed my own wicked heart that participation in the redeeming work of intercession becomes possible. It is then that the power to change history is released through prayer.

"Elijah was a man with a nature like ours, and he prayed earnestly that it would not rain; and it did not rain on the land for three years and six months. And he prayed again, and the heaven gave rain, and the earth produced its fruit" (Jas. 5:17,18, *NKJV*).

As we stand in the gap for America, we allow the Holy Spirit to shine the bright light of truth into the inner rooms of our souls. We run from the religious deceit that would seduce us into believing that we are superior to any person. It is only by the blood of the Lamb and the power of the Spirit that we stand free from the chains of guilt and the sentence of death.

This is why I stood and wept before the Maoris of New Zealand in 1990. I am not superior to my own ancestors. In my own way, I had participated in the same kinds of sins. God sees it that way, and unless I see the truth of it, He cannot use me in the ministry of reconciliation, either in reconciling people to Himself as an evangelist, or to each other as a peacemaker.

"Woe is me, for I am undone!
Because I am a man of unclean lips,
And I dwell in the midst of a people of unclean lips;
For my eyes have seen the King,
The Lord of hosts" (Isa. 6:5, *NKJV*).

■ ■ ■

Notes
1. Mark A. Wall, "The Puzzling Faith of Abraham Lincoln," *Christian History* magazine, Issue 33, Vol. XI, No. 1.
2. Ibid.

8

HOW DID HE
GET IN HERE?

In This Way We Are Wounded

A wounded spirit who can bear?

Proverbs 18:14 *(KJV)*

The incident took place at the mines near the gritty industrial town of Birmingham, Alabama. After months of verbal conflict with the United Mine Workers (UMW), the agents of the Bardeleben Coal Corporation planted dynamite on the road leading to the coal camp and mounted machine guns to keep out organizers. Finally, in October 1934, a full-scale gunfight involving some 1500 striking miners and company guards resulted in one man being killed and many wounded.

It was also another wound in the American body, another set of memories poisoned with hatred and mistrust.

Henry De Bardeleben Jr. was absolutely determined to keep his mining empire out of the UMW, and he succeeded. Like many of his social contemporaries, he saw life as a ruthless competition with all of the spoils to the victor. He was a practical, no-nonsense man, akin to Cornelius Vanderbilt, J. P. Morgan or Henry Ford. Like them, he glorified the competitive spirit and man's mastery of nature and debunked education and history. His father, Henry F. De Bardeleben, once said, "Life is one big game of poker." Surveying his vast domain of 15,000 acres of mining lands, he boasted, "I was the eagle, and I wanted to eat all the crawfish I could—swallow up all the little fellows, and I did it!"[1]

Such men exemplify a recurring perversion of the American dream—men who have gloried in economic competition, not for the sake of service to the nation or even productivity and wealth, but with a predator's lust to conquer and ingest. Their actions helped to push the nation into two equally self-righteous camps, shouting accusations at each other from the left and from the right. It is when America is polarized in this way that we suffer our deepest wounds.

I wonder what William Bradford, Jonathan Edwards and our other spiritual forefathers would think of the teeming complicated land that emerged through revolution and survived the Civil War. In spite of the vast cultural diversity of today's America, I think that men like Edwards would still point us to God's dealings with Israel as the model for the Christian remnant within America today.

The Cleansing and Healing of Israel

Ezekiel 22 is a proclamation of judgment upon Israel. "You have become guilty by the blood which you have shed, and defiled by your idols which you have made" (v. 4). "Behold, then, I smite My hand at your dishonest gain which you have acquired and at the bloodshed which is among you" (v. 13).

The prophet points to the violation of the covenant found

in Deuteronomy 27. "The alien they have oppressed in your midst; the fatherless and the widow they have wronged in you" (Ezek. 22:7), and goes on to proclaim: "You are a land that is not cleansed or rained on in the day of indignation" (v. 24).

"The people of the land have practiced oppression and committed robbery, and they have wronged the poor and needy and have oppressed the sojourner without justice" (v. 29).

The holy nature of God is deeply offended by Israel's behavior. He hates sin. He hates the agony it causes; there must be intervention for the sake of future generations. The land must be cleansed, justice must be fulfilled. But is there hope for that defiled generation?

The compassion of God is also aroused. "And I searched for a man among them who should build up the wall and stand in the gap before Me for the land, that I should not destroy it; but I found no one. Thus I have poured out My indignation on them" (vv. 30,31).

This is one of the most commonly quoted passages when prayer leaders call for intercession. To "stand in the gap" (between God and man) is now the priestly role of the Church. We present the blood of Jesus before the Father for the sins of the land just as the ancient priesthood presented the blood of bullocks in making atonement for the land. But what of the preceding phrase "build up the wall"? What does that mean?

We find the same word picture when the false prophets are condemned in Ezekiel 13:4,5: "Oh Israel, your prophets have been like foxes among ruins. You have not gone up into the breaches, nor did you build the wall around the house of Israel to stand in the battle on the day of the Lord."

Think of Nehemiah's day. His task was to reconstruct Jerusalem architecturally, socially and spiritually. One priority was to repair the ancient gates, the legitimate places of entrance, authority and decision, with all of their covenantal significance. But what about the gaps in the walls? It was to these illegitimate gates that Sanballat and Tobiah came, operating in a spirit of accusation and deception. "Now it came about when Sanballat, Tobiah, the Arabs, the Ammonites, and the Ashdodites heard that the repair of the walls of Jerusalem went on, and that the breaches began to be closed, that they were very angry. And all of them conspired together to come and fight against Jerusalem and to cause a disturbance in it" (Neh. 4:7,8).

What would you have done? If I had been in Nehemiah's shoes I would probably have ordered an immediate military sortie against this harassment, but Nehemiah was wiser; his priority was wall building. Each builder had to wear his sword at his side, but he had to keep building. Nehemiah refused to be distracted from his primary task by the presence of the enemy. "'I am doing a great work and I cannot come down. Why should the work stop while I leave it and come down to you?'" (Neh. 6:3).

Are these the priorities of today's intercessors? Are we chasing the enemy or repairing the wall? Sure, we have authority to move demons around, but is this the main task?*

Let me use a word picture that could make this concept clearer. Imagine that you are a field worker in Queensland, Australia, harvesting sugar cane. You are cutting cane with a razor-sharp machete. The heat is oppressive; the air is full of flies. Salty sweat stings your eyes; the sun burns down; the blade bites into the cane.

As you bend into the next stroke, suddenly, an accident. The blade has glanced off a stalk and slashed a gaping wound in your left arm.

What do you do? Smelling blood, the flies are already swarming to your wound. It is their nature to do so.

---

*Have you noticed that demons are recycled rather than destroyed? Even in the ministry of Jesus they were relocated, with the possibility of return (see Luke 11:26). Apparently it is necessary that we face an adversary in this brief terrestrial apprenticeship in order to express the full potential of agape (sacrificial) love. (See chapter 12, "Born to Battle" in *Taking Our Cities for God* for further explanation.)

You could do one of two things:

Option A

Form a defensive posture and attack the flies with your blade. Keep them moving. Try to keep them away from your wound.

Option B

Get stitches in that thing! Cleanse and close that wound. Do everything that you can to promote healing, thus making the presence of the flies irrelevant.

For too long we have tried the spiritual equivalent of Option A. In the unseen realm, we have an enemy that swarms to wounds and corruption.

They Smell Blood

The Bible teaches that deliverance from demons is linked to healing. This is how it describes the ministry of Jesus. "And they brought to Him all sick people who were afflicted with various diseases and torments and those who were demon-possessed, epileptics, and paralytics; and He healed them" (Matt. 4:24, *NKJV*).

Note that three categories are mentioned:

- Afflictions of the body—*diseases*.
- Afflictions of the soul—*torments*.
- Afflictions of the spirit—*demons*.

Healed of demons? It sounds strange, but we can learn something here.

Let me tell you a story.

We rolled west through the red rock foothills toward the

desert. Next stop, Las Vegas. The sky was radiant turquoise and the summer heat beat down on the valley floor.

"Look, Dad," said one of the boys. "Vultures! Up high and circling!"

We all watched them through the van window, getting closer. "What does that tell us?" I asked.

"Something's dying out there, but it's not dead yet, or they would have stopped circling; they would have landed," said Paul.

"What would we do if we wanted to rescue it?" I asked.

"We wouldn't shoot the vultures, Dad. If we did that we wouldn't know how to find it," said Matt.

Matthew had a good point—one that gives us a picture of strategy in prayer. Out there in the desert was something wounded, something dying, something that needed revival. The circling presence of the vultures was like a finger in the sky pointing to the place that needed help.

When we look at this nation, we see places that have attracted great satanic oppression. They are places that repel light and export darkness. Believers have been equipped with the gift of discerning of spirits, sensitized by God to the presence of evil. The presence of the enemy actually points the way to the things that need attention.

Having discerned a stronghold, what do we do? First, let's look at how a stronghold is established.

Let's imagine a conversation between a ranking principality and a demon on this subject. Remember, its objective is to break relationships and grieve the Spirit of God.

The Nature of Strongholds

Instructions to a Demon

1. Take some truth.
2. Polarize the people with different sides of that truth.
3. Tempt them to unrighteous judgment.

4. Watch them wound each other with rejection, harsh words and injustice.
5. Now that they are alienated, resentful and feeling guilty, bring them under condemnation by accusing them and tormenting them with remorse. Recruit other demons. Attempt to establish a permanent stronghold.
6. In the midst of their pain and confusion, offer them a way out through a cover-up deception, a religion or philosophy that covers guilt through transferring blame to nature, matter or society. They can't live without hope. Give them a false hope.
7. Attempt to close the prison door by permanently damaging their knowledge of God's character. Above all else, bring accusation against God.

That's it reader. It's that simple and it's been going on since the Fall. Satan's methods never change. Most of the authority Satan's kingdom has gained has been obtained through this pattern of accusation and deception. Our vulnerability is our unresolved guilt and our broken relationships.

This world is hopelessly snared in irreconcilable differences. Rodney King's question is indeed *the* question of the decade: "Can we all get along?" The answer is *no*. Without Jesus it's impossible. All successful relationship is Trinitarian in nature. You, your husband and Jesus, then it will work. If there are just two of you, prepare for pain. You, your friend and Jesus. Two nations plus Jesus. Two genders plus Jesus. Jesus said, "'Apart from Me you can do nothing'" (John 15:5). Least of all show love.

This brings us back to the unique role of God's people in bringing reconciliation. We alone can effect reconciliation because we alone are free to be honest. We were reconciled to God through honest confession and we reconcile people to people in the same way.

Once a leading Pharisee named Nicodemus came alone to Jesus at night. He was a sincere man, an earnest man, and he began to ask Jesus penetrating questions. Jesus knew that no man knows how wicked he is until he tries to be righteous, so He cut right to the heart of things. In the midst of a dignified conversation, He used an illustration that must have sounded really crude upon first hearing. He said, "I say to you, 'Unless one is born again, he cannot see the kingdom of God'" (John 3:3). Nicodemus was flabbergasted. "How can a man be born when he is old? He cannot enter a second time into his mother's womb and be born, can he?" (John 3:4). Jesus' powerful word picture implied not only new beginnings, but also restored innocence. Next time you are at the mall, go up to a family with a newborn baby and look into its eyes. What do you see there? Malice? Shifty-eyed calculation, fear and envy? Of course not. You see innocence.

What Jesus was saying to Nicodemus was in effect, "How would you like to take a shower on the inside? How would you like to lay down between the sheets tonight with that mountain of unresolved guilt absolutely gone? How would you like to be as innocent as a newborn baby?"

Now, Jesus was alluding to His own work as Savior. He alone is the source of our salvation. But how do we come to Him? Every religion and philosophy in history deals with personal and corporate guilt by covering it up. The pagans can't afford to be honest. If they do not know the plan of salvation, self-deception is their only option. The truth is too devastating. All have sinned and "the wages of sin is death" (Rom. 6:23). That puts every unredeemed person on death row, without possibility of pardon. In order to survive psychologically, pagans must comfort themselves with some form of self-justification. They cannot live without hope. Some intellectual sleight of hand is used to transfer blame to either nature, matter or society, but we who come to Jesus have to come in stark honesty with nothing covered.

It might be extreme to say that sin only leaves the body through the mouth, but we all understand that a precondition of repentance is that we acknowledge to God and to ourselves who we really are and what we have done. It's similar to film coiled in the back of a camera. The negative image will always remain unless we pop the latch, open the cover, and let the light flood in. This first catharsis of honesty at conversion leads to a lifetime of honesty.

THE FREEDOM TO BE HONEST GIVES US GREAT POWER TO HEAL IN A WORLD FULL OF ALIENATION, WHERE PEOPLE THIRST FOR INTIMACY, YET REMAIN ISOLATED AND IMPRISONED BY FEAR AND PRIDE.

The Holy Spirit never lets us get away with anything; however, there is more at stake than our own cleansing. This freedom to be honest gives us great power to heal in a world full of alienation, where people thirst for intimacy, yet remain isolated and imprisoned by fear and pride. This is a world in which ancient animosities still fester, and new offenses take place every day. The Bible says, "And those from among you will rebuild the ancient ruins; you will raise up the age-old foundations; and you will be called the repairer of the breach, the restorer of the streets in which to dwell" (Isa. 58:12).

If we are to effect healing and reconciliation in today's polarized society, we first need to go back to the American story and see if we can discern where patterns of broken relationships have taken place. If Satan has found a point of entry, perhaps we in this generation can show him the exit.

■ ■ ■

9

TELL ME
WHERE IT HURTS

Acknowledging Our Wounds

*He heals the brokenhearted,
and binds up their wounds.*

Psalm 147:3

I first heard the thumping of chopper blades above my roof, then looking out the window saw an eery, orange light flickering on the buildings. The night was cut with restless human sounds and I decided to investigate. From the front door I could see it: blazing gasoline flames just beyond the last house. Something sinister was going on right next to our Youth With a Mission property.

Creeping toward the fire I suddenly felt as though I had entered a temple of malice. There in our "black neighborhood" stood the terrifying symbol of the white supremacists. Three huge crosses blazed against the night sky.

Twenty men, mostly dressed in Ku Klux Klan robes and

hoods, chanted racist slogans and raised their arms in Nazi-style salutes. A man stepped forward to pray. Peter Lake, a free-lance journalist who had infiltrated the group, later described what was said. "So long as the alien occupies your land, hate is your law and revenge is your first duty. We light these crosses in the name of our God, over the luciferian scum of the earth."[1] The man praying was the notorious Richard Butler, head of the Idaho-based Aryan Nations.

Standing in the shadows was the even more famous Tom Metzger, who has since lost a $12.5 million judgment, awarded to the family of a black man beaten to death by Oregon skin-heads allegedly inspired by Metzger. Former Grand Dragon of the California KKK, he now heads the White Aryan Resistance, which advocates separation of the races and claims that the Holocaust never happened. Also present was Stanley Witek, the head of the neo-Nazi party. Lake quoted the supremacist as saying, "Los Angeles has become a mongrel cesspool of people, in which whites had to assert themselves."[2]

That was a rainy night in December of 1983. Sixteen years ago I moved my family to the house we now own. As a white immigrant from distant New Zealand, I was almost completely ignorant of the deep divisions that exist in American life. Black musicians had been my heroes, so the prospect of living in a black community was exciting.

I began to work with a group called "Black Ministries Unlimited" in South Central Los Angeles. I was invited to teach, but I was the one who had the most to learn. Patient Afro-American Christians drew me into their lives and told me their stories; even now I am just beginning to understand. Since then I have become part of a black church in America with a huge network of relationships from coast to coast.

In Chicago and Detroit, Miami and Atlanta, the black community seems afflicted with a common spiritual oppression. Black believers have explained to me the unique nature of their spiritual battle, leading me to ask God about my own place of service.

I began to realize that even though my own neighborhood has made headlines many times, California's problems are largely an outgrowth of the black experience in the old South. The spiritual gates—the places of entrance, authority and decision— were the great slave auctions of places such as Charleston and Richmond. So my family and I have traveled; on one occasion for two and one-half months, from city to city, responding to the invitations of united pastors. I now carry 23 years of memories on the road in America. Let's look closely at one of the key cities.

> Birmingham is probably the most thoroughly segregated city in the United States. Its ugly record of police brutality is known in every section of this country. Its unjust treatment of Negroes in the courts is a notorious reality. There have been more unsolved bombings of Negro homes and churches in Birmingham than any city in this nation. These are the hard, brutal and unbelievable facts.[3]

So wrote Dr. Martin Luther King Jr. in his now-famous letter from the Birmingham city jail, April 16, 1963.

In the late 1980s, I met with an extensive cross section of Birmingham's Christian leadership at one of the city's leading Presbyterian churches. I was impressed by their beautiful city and their earnest desire to transcend painful memories and walk together in harmony. I presented a lecture on how God is using His people to heal our cities through identificational repentance, and asked them to consider the categories of human conflict that have opened wounds and made room for satanic authority in Birmingham. At the end of the day I was handed a raft of books, articles and research by believers who had already been doing homework on the subject. Most encouraging was a secular book by a history professor from Auburn University, Wayne Flint, which contained a list almost identical to my own.

The New Century

In some ways, Birmingham is a microcosm of the story of America since the Civil War. It is not a city of the old South. It emerged just after reconstruction at the place where railroad lines intersected.

The years following the Civil War belonged to industry and the railroad. Ribbons of steel pushed in all directions, connecting east to west and joining teeming cities with the agricultural hinterland. Iron and steel were needed for rolling stock, rail and locomotives, and men were needed to feed the giant furnaces with coal and coke. Initially, labor was so scarce that agents were sent to Europe to recruit workers for Birmingham's mills. Between 1900 and 1910, the population increased about 245 percent and Birmingham became the third most populous city in the former Confederacy.

The town was dominated by a class of entrepreneurs, heavily influenced by the new theories of social Darwinism. They attributed their success to genetic superiority (the "survival of the fittest"), and they saw labor as an underclass of unfortunates who were to be "worked like hell" until they were no longer useful. The upheaval of the Civil War had permanently changed the old agricultural system and eventually resulted in an avalanche of freedmen and poor whites into the city.

The homogeneous blend of native-born Baptists and Methodists, Protestants common to the south, was replaced by great diversity. The religious census of 1906 revealed that the largest single denomination was Roman Catholic—28 percent, and that the city included populations of Jews and Greek-

Orthodox Christians. The second largest group was national Baptists (black) — 14.6 percent.

By 1915, the number of poor whites pouring into the town had produced a politically conscious Protestant majority determined to impose their moral values on the city's scandalous public life. This meant children should be in school, not factories; saloons and brothels should be closed; political corruption should be eliminated; and blacks should be disenfranchised. This clash between cultures at the beginning of the new century produced a rash of religious and ethnic violence.

In 1916, night riders burned a Catholic church and school. Weeks later arsonists destroyed two public schools and rumors swept the city that Catholics had done it in retaliation. By 1920, anti-Catholicism had reached a crescendo. The newspapers of the time reveal a Baptist pastor, R. L. Durant, trading diatribe and rebuttal with Father James E. Coyle of St. Paul's Catholic Church. On August 11, 1921, the cycle of bigotry reached a violent climax when Methodist minister, E. R. Stevenson, a member of the Ku Klux Klan, shot Father Coyle to death as he sat on the front porch of St. Paul's parsonage after a wedding ceremony. Coyle had united in marriage Stevenson's daughter with a Catholic boy. Stevenson quickly won acquittal from a sympathetic jury.

One historian estimates that more than half the city's Protestant ministers either belonged to or sympathized with the Klan. In many cases, the Klan embraced an agenda the ministers favored: enforcement of prohibition; restoration of traditional moral values; an application of pressure to stop adultery, divorce, drunkenness, hooliganism and political corruption.

A few courageous ministers publicly spoke out against the Klan's tactics, but most were silent, as they would be 40 years later during Birmingham's racial agony. Then, as later, it was the business community acting in self-interest, which tried to expose and weaken the Klan and open dialogue between contending factions.

Birmingham perfectly fit the profile of a Klan town: A rapidly growing city in which whites felt that their jobs were threatened by blacks and aliens and that their culture was imperiled by Catholics, Jews, flappers and secularists.

One of the largest events in Alabama's history took place at East Lake Park in 1924. Forty thousand people witnessed the initiation of 4,000 new Klansmen. It ended with exploding fireworks and a parade of 5,000 local Klansmen in full regalia, escorted through the streets of Birmingham by a police motorcade and a band and drum corps.

The Klan and those seeing themselves as "true Americans" made it clear that they bitterly opposed alternative values and were determined to impose their own ways, by force if necessary. After the advent of racial segregation following 1900, neighborhoods became more defined. They tended to organize around common elements such as race, class, occupation, religion or language.

On top of all this, constant strife occurred between labor and management in local industry. Mining strikes in 1894, 1907, 1919 and 1920, together with periodic steel and textile workstoppages, frequently ended in violence. Owners and managers usually prevailed. I don't believe in "coddling workmen," said Colonel John C. Maben,[4] president of a company notorious for wretched working conditions.

The Wounds of America

The worst period of testing was the Great Depression of the 1930s, a period that revealed what Professor Wayne Flint calls the "stress fractures"[5] in the city's life. Flint mentions eight conditions in Birmingham that I find are common to the American experience and define our unfinished business to this day: class division; worker grievances; racial discord; lack of economic diversity; wretched housing; inadequate provision of public services; inadequate food and fuel; and destructive patterns of localism.

Do these fractures correspond to the spiritual strongholds we encounter in modern life? I think so. If we enlarge the list a little, we get something like this.

Places of Conflict and Broken Relationship

1. Race to Race (e.g., Native American vs. European American)
2. Class to Class (e.g. Homeless Person vs. Holders of Home Equity)
3. Culture to Culture (e.g., Immigrant vs. Native Born)
4. Gender to Gender (e.g., Working Woman vs. Male Hierarchy)
5. Vocation to Vocation (e.g., L.A. Police Department vs. Civil Rights Advocates)
6. Institution to Institution (e.g., Auto Industry Management vs. Organized Labor)
7. Region to Region (e.g., Westside vs. South Central L.A.)
8. Governed to Government (e.g., College-Age Youth vs. Vietnam Era Government)
9. Religion to Religion (e.g., Muslim vs. Christian)
10. Denomination to Denomination (i.e. Protestant vs. Catholic)
11. Enterprise to Enterprise (e.g., Monopoly vs. Small Business)
12. Idealogy to Idealogy (e.g., Leftist vs. Rightist Political Parties)

13. Nationality to Nationality (e.g., Americans vs. Cubans)
14. Generation to Generation (e.g., '60s Youth vs. Parents
15. Family to Family (e.g., Neighbor vs. Neighbor)

This list could be endlessly refined. However, we need something this basic as a guide in order to begin our journey toward national healing.

■ ■ ■

Notes

1. Tracy Wilkinson, *Los Angeles Times*, Tuesday, October 29, 1991.
2. Ibid.
3. Martin Luther King Jr., *Why We Can't Wait* (New York: Harper-Collins, 1963, 1964), p. 290. The American Friends Committee first published this essay as a pamphlet.
4. Wayne Flint, *Building a New South City: Leadership Patterns in Birmingham's History* (Birmingham, AL: Leadership Birmingham, 1988), p. 26.
5. Ibid., pp. 27, 31.

10

DUTY, HONOR, COUNTRY—1999

The Christian and the Nation-State

And I saw another angel flying in midheaven, having an eternal gospel to preach to those who live on the earth, and to every nation and tribe and tongue and people.

Revelation 14:6

I saw him standing at the back. Young, wearing an over-sized green jacket and blue jeans; a mop of brown hair and a pale face. When the lecture finished he approached me. "I want to show you something," he said.

Later that day this earnest, young German took me to the site of a concentration camp. My friend Bob was with me. He was a Vietnam veteran from Fort Worth, Texas. Driving back from the camp we were silent; the ghastly images were too profound to explore in conversation.

Suddenly our host turned and confronted Bob. "Why did you fight in Vietnam?"

"Duty, honor and country," said Bob.

"That's what my father believed," snapped the young man. "He lost his arm at the siege of Stalingrad."

Obviously angry, he changed direction and drove furiously down side streets until we arrived at a modest home. Stamping up the front steps he burst through the door and beckoned us to come in. Inside were his parents, a gracious older couple who offered us coffee. An empty sleeve dangled at his father's left side.

"Your son has been showing us around," I said.

"He loves to do that," said the boy's mother. "Where did he take you?"

"To the concentration camp," blurted the boy, and her face fell.

"Why can't you show them something good about Germany?" was her anguished complaint.

This young man was a devout Christian who spent his summers organizing bus tours to the still-intact Nazi death camps, preserved as monuments by the communist government of Poland. He saw the state as something intrinsically evil that must be constantly opposed by Christian activists. My American friend Bob saw his nation as basically good and worthy of Christian loyalty. It was interesting to listen to them argue. At the root of their contention with each other was a basic question: What is the role of believers within the nation-state?

Redemptive Gifts

Peoples, cultures and nations have a redemptive purpose because they bear God-created gifts. They all have a power to bless the world that is an outgrowth of their unique attributes. All that exists is created by God. Satan has never created, and holds no title deed to anything: he is only a creature. God is love, therefore, all that is created serves His ultimate loving purpose: that love be poured out on His creation, and that loving relationship be multiplied throughout time and eternity.

Everything created has a purpose, although every purpose is not yet fully understood. Purpose can and will be revealed by our loving Creator, if the knowledge gained will be used lovingly. God's most majestic and important creation is humankind. We are destined for the throne, having the potential of becoming the bride of Christ. We are made in God's own image; therefore, something of God's own nature is revealed through our creation.

God commanded Adam and Eve to be fruitful and multiply, there being a need for hundreds of millions of us to become the expanding scope for the revelation of God's nature, character and personality. (There has never been a person exactly like you before and there never will be.) However, there is a division of labor within this task.

God Himself is the ultimate Author of the diversity of human characteristics. This diversity ranges from the individual to the nation-state, or even a linguistic family of nations. The initial division of labor is between male and female; and the next division of labor is given to the descendants of the progenitors Ham, Shem and Japheth: "From these the whole earth was populated" (Gen. 9:19).

Redemptive Purpose

The peoples of the earth have all been created with the purpose of worshiping God uniquely and contributing unique service to other peoples. These diverse gifts bring power to serve or to dominate, to wound or to heal, and God judges or blesses each people group according to their moral state as He works His redemptive purpose in the seasons of human history. "But the plans of the Lord stand firm forever, the purposes of his heart through all generations" (Ps. 33:11, *NIV*).

As it is with nations and peoples, so it is with individuals. The identity of the individual is based on his or her uniqueness or difference, which is the basis of his or her beauty and value. These distinctions can be seen by simply looking at the categories we currently fall into and exploring their potential. This list would include: gender, generation, language, nationality, race, culture, class, family, location, vocation, appearance, personality and gifting. We all need revelation about God's purpose for us at every level. This is the basis of our sense of destiny.

The discovery of purpose for this uniqueness brings hope to the individual or the nation-state or anything else in between. The person, ideology or institution bringing the greatest hope gains the greatest authority to lead others into the future. However, only those in a position to receive revelation from the Creator are able to proclaim true purpose.

Desperate Questions About Identity

We live in a world absolutely bewildered by the counterclaims of religion, race, culture and nationality. The borders imposed by the former communist and colonial empires are proving to be fragile. Redrawing the maps of Europe, Central Asia, the Middle East and Africa could be the source of mindless savagery for decades to come. Even the more stable multiethnic experiments such as the United States, the United Kingdom and Canada are feeling the strains of a new era. The American of the 1950s knew that ethnicity melted away in the New World as immigrants faced the inebriating effects of freedom, democracy and rock and roll. Instead, today we are experiencing an atomization into tribes and subcultures, each with its own notion of sovereignty.

The civilizing, law-providing functions of the nation-state have become more tenuous. Definitions of family, justice and transcendent truth are up for grabs. Some radicals have taken multiculturalism beyond its original goal of giving dignity to all heritages and now call their followers into an irrational tribalism in which destructive lawlessness can be justified as the insurrection of an oppressed people. Perhaps the deepest separation between us derives not from race or ethnicity, but from class. To put matters bluntly, the black executive has more in common culturally with her Hispanic, Asian or white colleagues than she does with the gang kids of Pacoima or South Central Los Angeles. This is why white, middle-class kids are infatuated with lower-class black style. Ghetto talk, gestures, dress, defiance and swagger have become the vehicle for expressing rebellion against authority in the suburbs.

As the influence of religion and traditional values has declined, a new doctrine of self-actualization has emerged, promoting a therapeutic culture that promises fulfillment without sacrifice, redemption with no strings attached. Psychotherapists teach us that we are all victims, unable to take responsibility for our own actions. And lawyers seem to tell us there is always somebody to sue.

Some ethnic leaders promote victimization as a source of power and moral superiority. Such influence is transforming the civil rights movement from an effort to win equality under the law into an industry dedicated to winning special treatment for victims. Warning against this, Martin Luther King Jr. said, "We must not let the fact that we are victims of injustice lull us into abrogating the respect for our own lives."[1]

Some champions of culture would like to endow ordinary internal differences within a society—of gender, race and cultural pattern—with the inflated character of nationhood. Does this mean that ethnic groups, desiring to preserve their heritage, should compel women to wear veils, toss themselves onto their husband's funeral pyres or submit to polygamy? Should cultural pluralism be accompanied by moral relativism? Is any behavior permissible as long as there is some culture or subculture that permits it?

It was on these grounds that two Palestinian emigrés, who had murdered their Americanized teenage daughter, asked for acquittal. A friend said, "We follow our religion." If these parents hadn't disciplined their wayward daughter, "they'd be embarrassed in front of everybody." In short: "It's a Palestinian thing. You wouldn't understand."

Where does that kind of reasoning lead us? Was Ivan Boesky's insider trading just a "rich thing"? Is mob crime just a "Costa Nostra thing"? Maybe looting is a "poverty thing—you wouldn't understand." Radical feminists have made this kind of claim in sanctioning abortion. One prominent feminist, recently quoted in a national newspaper, suggested that a feminine approach to moral questions has developed that is clearly distinct from the masculine. She argues that for women, abstract absolutes of right and wrong, even individual rights, are less important than concern with caring, responsibility and the concrete realities of a given situation—the context. She suggests we need to ask if the fetus is economically viable, given the circumstances of the mother, the family and the community. And goes on to suggest one more question: Is it culturally viable?

What in the world does "cultural viability" mean as a standard by which human life should be terminated or continued? If we have no uniting standards of morality, people will not only think they can get away with anything, but they will also believe they are *entitled* to get away with anything. By declaring that there are hundreds of separate moral systems within America, all perfectly acceptable, proponents of such relativism strike at the heart of the American social covenant in a way that cultural relativism does not.

Should ethnic Americans step away from the mainstream or claim their place in it? Should each subculture rally around the single quality that makes them different from the "blonde beast" of popular imagination—the mythical white male—and pursue power based on that quality? Will the majority of people once termed "minority" reject the cult of romanticized ethnocentrism and continue in a spirit of common agreement about what America is to be, or will we degenerate into bickering factions? Can there be diversity within our unity? And what about the Church? Where are God's people in all this? Do we have wisdom for a nation in crisis?

A nation without a uniting vision will cease to be a nation. This is not always a bad thing—consider the collapse of the Soviet Union. However, a people must define an identity at some level and base their lives on more than just ethnicity or language. There is a loving ambition in the heart of God to bless the whole human family with distinct inheritances.

> "Remember the days of old,
> Consider the years
>   of many generations.
> Ask your father, and he will show you;
> Your elders, and they will tell you:
> When the Most High divided their
>   inheritance to the nations,
> When He separated the sons of Adam,
> He set the boundaries of the peoples"
> (Deut. 32:7,8, *NKJV*).

A Theology of Nations

Imagine humankind living in a world without sin. What kind of communities would have arisen if the Fall had not occurred? In an unfallen state, the gifts that came to expression in human culture, the arts, technology, architecture and craftsmanship would have developed to a superb level. Adam was commanded to cultivate the earth's resources and build with the things placed at his disposal. He was to organize and govern, under God, the world in which God placed him. As the human family expanded, the nation-state as we know it may never have emerged, but there certainly would have been multigenerational family extension with resulting territoriality and cultural uniqueness. The nations that emerged would have been theocentric, covenant peoples, honoring God by perfect obedience and benefiting their inhabitants in every way.

The Bible describes in Revelation 21 an aspect of the kingdom of God that is yet to unfold. The holy city, the New Jerusalem, is beautiful beyond description, unblemished by sin. Death and mourning are gone; there is no pain or tears; God dwells with His people in perfect relationship; a redeemed people are drawn by grace from every race, nation and language group.

Between the lost opportunity of humanity before the Fall and the Kingdom that has not yet come in fullness, stand the nations that now exist. Because of sin, they are human-centered, contentious and filled with imperfection, but things are not as bad as they might be. By God's mercy, even the most pagan nations still reflect some of the image of God. Sin and evil are at work, but, because of God's grace, there is virtue and beauty and demonic potentials are restrained along with the worst intentions of evil people.

The nations as they are represent an adaptation to the fallen condition of their citizens; they are evidence of God's preserving and preventative grace. In mercy, God has appointed nations to restrain the course of humankind's self-destructive potential. Imagine if the world were united under one central government and the system became utterly corrupted. There would be no nations of refuge to run to (Jesus found shelter in Egypt as a child), no independent states that could form a righteous alliance against tyranny.

The nations we know today are not to be identified with

either the kingdom of God or the kingdom of Satan. They are transitory structures in which two separate kingdoms vie for supremacy, with two sets of citizens living by two different standards.

Christians are not humanistic idealists, filled with utopian schemes for the creation of a perfect society. We understand our nations to be temporary, and to some degree under the curse, but we are involved in a fierce battle for human minds and hearts within the shelter of national structures. We, therefore, create useful institutions, promote justice, pray for the national welfare and stand as a hedge against evil supernatural powers.

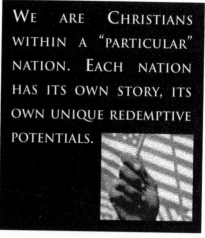

WE ARE CHRISTIANS WITHIN A "PARTICULAR" NATION. EACH NATION HAS ITS OWN STORY, ITS OWN UNIQUE REDEMPTIVE POTENTIALS.

However, there is more to it than that. We are Christians within a "particular" nation. Each nation has its own story, its own unique redemptive potentials.

How is a uniting national dream to be discovered? Many nations have their image disseminated by a government tourism department or their identity defined by a state-supported ideology such as Castro's Cuba or the Ayatollah's Iran. In the absence of revelation from God, deception finds credibility. This is not a new problem. It was faced by many biblical reformers following a period of apostasy in Israel's history.

Consider the life of Daniel. Through this steadfast prophet, Israel received three essential types of information necessary for national recovery. The same could be said for the ministry of Ezra, Nehemiah and many others.

1. God's perspective on the past. Israel's broken covenants

and unclaimed promises. How they got into their present predicament.
2. Steps of obedience for today's generation. The plan for restoration.
3. Revelation about Israel's purpose as a nation among nations. Prophetic promises that would bring hope to generations of Israelites yet unborn.

This is exactly the information we need about America. Repentance and humble inquiry will lead to its release. It may be that as we cleanse our temple we will find this revelational information already written down somewhere, such as the young King Josiah (see 2 Kings 22,23; 2 Chron. 34,35), or perhaps the travail of the intercessor will bring to birth new understanding.

Can We Be Trusted?

One of the greatest examples of travail is the prayer life of Daniel. The book of Daniel gives graphic accounts of war in the heavenlies. However, the most interesting story is God's dealings with His servant. Let's look closely at this process.

Accusation and deception are Satan's only weapons; both are dependant on absent knowledge or distorted knowledge. Spiritual battles are often battles to see truth revealed, because, as God said through His prophet, "My people are destroyed for lack of knowledge" (Hos. 4:6).

If we are being destroyed for lack of knowledge, why doesn't God just tell us what we need to know? The problem is, "knowledge puffeth up" (1 Cor. 8:1, KJV) and God has promised the individual that He will "not allow you to be tempted beyond what you are able...to endure" (1 Cor. 10:13).

No temptation is more seductive to the human heart than

spiritual pride; nothing is more intoxicating than the delicious sense of having an insider's knowledge of the supernatural realm. This is why we see Daniel waiting for 21 days (see Dan. 10:13). God was testing and purifying His servant before placing upon him the weight of understanding about God's purpose for his nation.

I believe this is the season the American Church has entered. This is to be a sober, vigilant season, in which a praying, fasting Church qualifies to inherit knowledge. God wants to use this nation as a blessing to all nations. This is a land of refuge, outreach and example; however, the American Church has lost its voice, and this is in part because we do not know what to say.

God's people are the only legitimate channel for understanding national identity and national purpose because they alone enjoy unbroken communication with the Creator. If we do not speak out a godly dream for this nation, the ship of state will lose its rudder and drift with any wind.

I have already hinted at what I think the gift of this land has been, and is to be, and we will explore the role of a land of refuge as we go along. It is sufficient to say here that it is not impossible for a people from diverse origins to find a common destiny. The principle of diversity within a union runs right through Creation up to the Trinitarian nature of God's own being.

An Unmarried Land

God spoke an unusual promise over Israel through the prophet Isaiah: "But you will be called 'My delight is in her,' and your land 'Married'; for the Lord delights in you, and to Him your land will be married. For as a young man marries a virgin, so your sons will marry you" (Isa. 62:4,5).

America is yet an unmarried land. It has many disparate,

scattered parts that are not yet fully joined together. The process is familiar enough: observation, attraction, courtship, covenant, intimacy, fruitfulness and celebration. Yes, there is something beyond reconciliation and healing, it is the destiny and purpose that becomes possible when a people are truly united. However, the nation can only tread the path that the Church has cleared. We must demonstrate unity in the midst of our own denominational and cultural diversity. We must show the way. Have we done that?

When I look at the Church of America, I see a people who sometimes mirror, more than they contrast, the national condition. In some cases, our greatest national sins are most deeply institutionalized within the Church. Consider the fact that Sunday is still the most racially segregated day of the week, and that some denominations still bear names that reflect a pro-slavery foundation. In spite of all this, I have great hope.

A new generation has emerged since World War II. I believe that even generations have a redemptive purpose. We have been served for many years, both in religion and politics, by those who were tested in the fires of a world at war. George Bush is typical of that generation—a fighter pilot who survived many missions; he is part of a generation whose style is heroic, sacrificial and combative.

President Clinton is the first of the new generation and, for better or for worse, we are in for change. Some unusual things have already begun to happen. Consider this. The U.S. Senate has just voted, 65 to 34, to issue a formal apology to native Hawaiians for the overthrow of their island kingdom by United States agents a century ago. The Senators urged the president "to provide a proper foundation for reconciliation between the United States and the native Hawaiian people."

The post-World War II baby boom is characterized by a longing for community. This was chronicled in music as the transition took place from the single idol (Elvis) to the group (the Beatles). As the boyish charm of the early Beatles disintegrated into drug abuse and contention, it was like watching a generation lose its most hopeful icon. Yet the anarchy and excess of the '60s still expressed the generational trait. What did young people do when they rebelled? They joined a commune. The James Dean type—a rebel without a cause—was left behind by the rebels with a cause, people dreaming about turning the whole earth into a giant family gathering, people on their way to a mythical Woodstock.

The end of this quest was, of course, total disillusionment, but if you scratch beneath the surface hardness of a boomer, you will find that the yearning still remains. After all, which came first, the message or the men? It was the children born in the decades before or after 1957* who carried this God-created redemptive trait—an unusual yearning for reconciliation—and now they have entered their season of leadership.

I speak as a 42-year-old when I say that our children will have grace for their own task. We, however, have been deeply sensitized by God to the wounds that exist between men and women, Afro-Americans and white Americans, and Native Americans and the legacy of Columbus. Enormous grace is flowing from the throne of God right now for the enabling of any believer who will approach these three arenas of conflict and pain.

■ ■ ■

Note

1. Jonathan Karl, "Everyone's a Victim, No One's Responsible," *The Wall Street Journal,* Monday, September 14, 1992.

---

* The peak year for births following World War II was 1957; baby boomers were born from 1946-1964.

PART III

REPAIRER OF THE BREACH

Healing America's Wounds

"And those from among you will rebuild the ancient ruins; you will raise up the age-old foundations; and you will be called the repairer of the breach, the restorer of the streets in which to dwell."

Isaiah 58:12

11

LET'S DO IT

The Story of the Reconciliation Coalition

God...reconciled us to himself through Christ and gave us the ministry of reconciliation.

2 Corinthians 5:18 *(NIV)*

My friends and I have a dream. We call it the International Reconciliation Coalition. Chapters have begun to form worldwide, dealing with conflict in a Christian way. We believe in confession, repentance, reconciliation and restitution. Let's define these terms.

> **CONFESSION:** Stating the truth; acknowledgment of the unjust or hurtful actions of myself or my people group toward other persons or categories of persons. (The main theme of this book because it is the place to begin and we have neglected it.)
> **REPENTANCE:** Turning from unloving to loving actions.

RECONCILIATION: Expressing and receiving forgiveness, and pursuing intimate fellowship with previous enemies.

RESTITUTION: Attempting to restore that which has been damaged or destroyed, and seeking justice wherever we have power to act or to influence those in authority to act.

The Judeo-Christian ethos present in this nation's roots gives us hope. During the great seasons of revival, the Christian community has always placed considerable emphasis on open acknowledgment of sin and called for changed attitudes and just actions. That is why this nation has the potential to demonstrate a model of reconciliation in the troubled world of the 1990s and beyond. We need to live up to this potential.

The chapters of the Coalition organize events and ceremonies in which representatives of offended subcultures or representatives of offending subcultures have an opportunity to express regret and/or extend forgiveness. We recognize that the human story is filled with complex issues and that today's generation has inherited the task of both honoring righteous ancestors and seeking forgiveness for ancestral sins.

It is our hope that our children will not have to deal with the hatred and alienation that have marked the experience of this and past generations. Our inclination is to uncover the ancient and modern wounds of injustice, pride and prejudice and to heal them in a biblical way—that is to say without self-righteous accusation or dishonest cover-up. Let's take a look at some reconcilers in action.

How the West Was Won

The shameful history of the United States' relationship with

Native Americans is becoming the focus of prayer networks all over the nation, and the Native American Affairs chapter, led by Jean Steffanson of Colorado, has become a clearinghouse for information among concerned intercessors. Solemn assemblies have begun to take place, not just in churches, but also at the actual places where negative events took place.

In November 1992, such an assembly was held at Confluence Park, the birthplace of Denver. The event was attended by politicians, pastors and representatives of the Native American peoples of the front range. This was followed in January 1993, by a gathering of Christians of all races at a remote massacre site near the town of Chivington, Colorado. Events took place there in the 1860s that are a major cause of bitterness and rejection of Christianity by increasing numbers of young Native Americans.

For many years, I have been listening to the hearts of Native American friends and the incident at Sand Creek always comes up. Most Americans have heard about the massacre at Wounded Knee in South Dakota, but few know anything about what occurred at Sand Creek, Colorado. The fact remains that it is one of the most important spiritual gates in this nation.

In November 1864, southern Cheyenne and Arapaho, wanting peace and being assured that they were under the protection of the state, were told to camp at Sand Creek, land within the area of the Fort Laramie Treaty of 1851. While most of the men were away hunting food for their families, the U.S. Army Colorado Volunteers, under the command of a Methodist preacher—one Colonel John Chivington—rushed in with more than 700 cavalry and opened fire at dawn. The result was 105 women and children and 28 men were dead. The atrocities did not stop there; the dead were mutilated in the worst ways; survivors and body parts were displayed from town to town. The military was commended rather than condemned for this action. No form of redress of grievance has ever been made and the events themselves are usually misreported, not as a massacre, but as a battle having legitimate cause.

Some background: In 1851, representatives of the United States government parleyed at Fort Laramie with a large encampment of Arapahos, Sioux, Cheyennes, Crows and other tribes. The result was a treaty in which the Plains Indians did not relinquish any rights or claims to their lands, but permitted the Americans to establish roads and military posts across their territory. Both parties swore "to maintain good faith and friendship in all their mutual intercourse, and to make an effective and lasting peace."[1]

Ten years later, white men flooded the Platte Valley and began to stake out ranches on territory assigned to southern Cheyennes and Arapahos. The Pikes Peak gold rush of 1858 had loosed an irreversible tide. Land that had once teemed with buffalo was forever changed. In spite of all this, the Cheyennes and Arapahos kept the peace.

Eventually, a new treaty was proposed and several chiefs from both tribes met with United States representatives at Fort Wise on the Arkansas River. The contents of the treaty as written were quite different from the verbal assurances given to the Indians. It was the understanding of the chiefs that they would gain a home territory and have freedom of movement throughout the region for the purpose of hunting wild game. A Cheyenne chief named Black Kettle was among the signers; two United States cavalry officers witnessed the signatures, John Sedgwick and J. E. B. Stewart (later to distinguish himself as a Confederate hero).

In 1863, Black Kettle and Lean Bear had been invited to Washington, where they personally met with Abraham Lincoln, who gave them each a medal. In the spring of 1864, they traveled to Fort Larned, Kansas, and were presented with a huge United States Garrison flag by Colonel Greenwood. Greenwood told Black Kettle that as long as he flew the flag above him no soldier would ever fire upon him. From that day on, he always mounted his flag above his tepee when in camp.

In May of that year, Black Kettle and Lean Bear were moving north to join other Cheyenne, when an advance party of hunters ran into soldiers equipped with cannons approaching the camp. When this was reported, Lean Bear put on his medal, took some papers that had been given him in Washington, and rode out with an escort to parley with the bluecoats. He saw four columns of cavalry approaching with two cannons in the center and wagons grouped to the rear.

Lean Bear left his warriors and rode out alone to shake hands with the officer and show the papers that certified that he was a good friend of the United States. When he was within 20 yards of the line of soldiers, the officer gave command and they all opened fire. Wounded, Lean Bear fell off his horse in front of the soldiers and was shot to death on the ground. The result was a confused melee, in which several white men and warriors were killed. In the midst of the fighting, Black Kettle appeared and tried to make peace. He rode up and down on his horse shouting, "Stop the fighting, do not make war!"[2] This action prevented the slaughter of this group of 100 soldiers by the now enraged Cheyenne, who counted more than 500 skilled warriors in their band.

Black Kettle was totally bewildered. Unknown by him at the time, Lieutenant George S. Eayre was under orders from Colonel John M. Chivington to "kill Cheyennes whenever and wherever found."[3] The white community was inflamed by exaggerated newspaper accounts of Indian raids—reports that made no distinction between the various tribes. The settlers wanted protection and they clamored for action from the army. Fear had cast out love.

Fearing the outbreak of a general war, Black Kettle restrained his warriors and sent his white friend, William Bent, to Fort Lyon, bearing the message that he wanted to be "friendly and peaceable and keep my tribe so. I am not able to fight the whites. I want to live in peace."[4] Bent met with Chivington but was rebuffed.

In June of the same year, John Evans, the governor of the Colorado territory, issued an edict to the effect that all Cheyennes and Arapahos should report to Fort Lyon in order to be furnished with provisions by Samuel G. Colley, the Indian agent. Indians not so gathered would be considered hostile and would be subdued by the U.S. Army. Various bands were scattered across western Kansas for the summer hunts, and weeks went by before news of the directive reached them. Numerous small clashes between Indians and soldiers took place. Sioux warriors from the Dakotas, aroused by punitive army expeditions into their territory, began to raid the wagon trains and settlements along the Platte at this time, and southern Cheyennes and Arapahos received much of the blame.

Black Kettle remained deeply disturbed by the escalating violence and did everything he could to make peace. When he discovered that two white women and five children had been captured in raids, he ransomed four of them from the captors with his own ponies so that he could return them safely. He contacted Colley for instructions on safe passage to the fort in compliance with Governor Evans's orders. He did not suspect that the Indian agent was deeply involved with the scheme hatched by the governor and Colonel Chivington to drive the Plains Indians from Colorado.

The commanding officer at Fort Lyon was a young man in his mid-20s named Edward Wynkoop. In this man, Black Kettle and the Indians found a friend. After listening to the Indians' side of the story of recent events, he promised to help negotiate peace and he traveled with several chiefs, including Black Kettle, all the way to Denver (400 miles) to seek an audience with the governor. At first Evans would not meet with Wynkoop, saying that the Cheyennes and Arapahos should be punished before giving them peace. When Wynkoop begged the governor to meet with the Indians, his response was, "What shall I do with the Third Colorado Regiment if I make peace? They have been raised to kill Indians and they must kill Indians."[5] Behind this statement was the reality of political pressure on Evans from Coloradans who wanted to avoid the Civil War military draft of 1864 by serving in uniform against a few poorly armed Indians, rather than fighting Confederate soldiers.

Eventually, Evans and Chivington met with the chiefs at Camp Weld. The chiefs pled for peace and explained in detail what had happened in various incidents, including the role of the Sioux raiders. Bull Bear said, "My brother Lean Bear died in trying to keep peace with the whites. I am willing to die the same way, and expect to do so.[6]

The council ended inconclusively when Chivington, a former Methodist preacher who had devoted his time to organizing Sunday Schools in the mining camps, rose to his feet and recommended that since the Indians felt safe with Major Wynkoop, they could go and camp near him at Fort Lyon. This they did, making camp at Sand Creek, about 40 miles northeast of the fort.

Wynkoop's friendly dealings with the Indians resulted in a reprimand and he was replaced by Major Scott J. Anthony, an officer of Chivington's Colorado Volunteers. Anthony's first action was to cut rations and demand the surrender of weapons. Disturbed by this, Black Kettle journeyed in from Sand Creek, but was assured by the major that his tribe was under the protection of the fort and that the warriors could go east and hunt buffalo until Anthony secured permission from the army to issue winter rations. Reassured by these words, the chiefs abandoned their plan to flee to the south and decided to remain at Sand Creek for the winter. Anthony now reported his intentions to his superiors. "I shall try to keep the Indians quiet until such time as I receive reinforcements."[7]

The reinforcements eventually arrived in the form of Chivington and 600 men of the Colorado Volunteers. Chivington immediately began talking of "collecting scalps" and "wading in gore." Anthony was enthusiastic; however, three of his officers were sickened by the well-planned massacre and wanted no part of it. Lieutenant James Conner stated that it would be a violation of a solemn pledge of safety and "it would be murder in every sense of the word," bringing dishonor to the uniform of the U.S. Army. Chivington's angry response was, "Damn any man who sympathizes with the Indian! I have come to kill Indians, I believe it is right and honorable to use any means under God's heaven to kill Indians."[8] The three officers were threatened with court-martial if they did not join the expedition. However, they quietly resolved to order their men not to fire their weapons except in self-defense. At eight o'clock on the evening of November 28, the column of soldiers moved out.

■ ■ ■

January 14, 1993: After days of wind, the morning broke clear and a warm sun shone on the line of cars crawling across the vastness. A shallow snow capped everything. We pulled up at the marker and stared down the side road tentatively—it was just a line of wheel ruts in the sand.

"You white people need to realize that you are direct beneficiaries of this massacre," said one of the Indian pastors.

This was confirmed to me in a hauntingly personal way. The man who owned the land was named Dawson and was a Baptist, which is what I am. We paid the man and continued on to the site.

A horseshoe bluff overlooks a few gnarled trees growing in a dry streambed. The rest of the prairie is empty. The atmosphere is one of deep solemnity. It is like standing next to a well of sorrows. We gather on the bluff in a circle, heads bowed. "Tell us what happened here," said Jean Steffanson, addressing the Indian leaders and those who had done research.

■ ■ ■

Notes

1. Dee Brown, *Bury My Heart at Wounded Knee* (New York: Simon & Schuster, 1970), p. 68.
2. Ibid., p. 71.
3. Ibid., p. 73.
4. Ibid.
5. Ibid., p. 79.
6. Ibid., p. 82.
7. Ibid., p. 85.
8. Ibid.

12

THE

MASSACRE

For godly sorrow produces repentance to salvation, not to be regretted; but the sorrow of the world produces death.

2 Corinthians 7:10 *(NKJV)*

Altogether, about 600 Indians were gathered in the creek bed; Black Kettle's tepee was at the center of the encampment. The warriors were several miles to the east hunting buffalo. Of those remaining in the camp, two-thirds of the people were women and children, just as Major Scott J. Anthony had planned. The Indians kept no night watch, being confident of their safety. The first warning they had was the drumming of hooves on the sand at sunrise. All hell broke loose. Hundreds of people were screaming, shouting, desperately trying to organize their children; men were diving for their weapons or running to form a defense. George Bent, an eyewitness, describes what he saw.

I looked toward the chief's lodge and saw that Black Kettle had a large American flag tied to the end of a long lodge pole, and was standing in front of his lodge, holding the pole, with the flag fluttering in the gray light of winter dawn. I heard him call to the people not to be afraid, that the soldiers would not hurt them; then the troops opened fire from two sides of the camp.[1]

People ran toward the American flag and the white flag of surrender next to it. Many came from down the creek where the old chief, White Antelope, had his camp, until hundreds of Cheyenne women and children were gathered around Black Kettle's lodge. White Antelope himself, still confident in the flag's protection, ran toward the soldiers shouting, "Stop! Stop!" until shot down. Another chief, Left Hand, stood with his arms folded, saying he would not fight the white man because they were his friends. He was shot down. Robert Bent, a rancher riding unwillingly with Chivington as a guide, describes what happened.

I think there were thirty-five braves and some old men, about sixty in all...after the firing the warriors put the squaws and children together, and surrounded them to protect them. I saw five squaws under a bank for shelter. When the troops came up to them, they ran out and showed their persons to let the soldiers know that they were squaws and begged for mercy, but the soldiers shot them all. I saw one squaw lying on the bank, whose leg had been broken by a shell; a soldier came up to her with a drawn saber; she raised her arm to protect herself, when he struck, breaking her arm, she rolled over and raised her other arm, when he struck, breaking it, and then left her without killing her. There seemed to be indiscriminate slaughter of men, women and children. There were some thirty or forty squaws collected in a hole for protection; they sent out a little girl about six years old with a white flag on a stick. She had not proceeded but a few steps when she was shot and killed. All the squaws in that hole were afterwards killed and four or five bucks outside. The squaws offered no resistance. Everyone I saw dead was scalped. I saw one squaw cut open with an unborn child, as I thought, lying on her side. Captain Soule afterwards told me that such was the fact. I saw the body of White Antelope with his privates cut off, and I heard a soldier say he was going to make a tobacco pouch out of them. I saw one squaw whose privates had been cut out...I saw a little girl about five years of age who had been hid in the sand; two soldiers discovered her, drew their pistols and shot her, and then pulled her out of the sand by the arms. I saw a number of infants in arms, killed with their mothers.[2]

Bent's description of the soldiers' atrocities was corroborated by Lieutenant James Conner:

In going over the battlefield the next day I did not see a body of man, woman or child but was scalped and in many instances their bodies were mutilated in the most horrible manners.[3]

Miraculously, Black Kettle survived. Lack of discipline among the soldiers, combined with heavy drinking of whiskey during the night ride, made it possible for many Indians to escape in small groups across the plain, where they joined the men at the hunting camp. Wails of grief accompanied each new arrival. Every family had lost loved ones. Historian, Dee Brown, states:

In a few hours of madness at Sand Creek, Chivington
and his soldiers destroyed the lives or the power of
every Cheyenne and Arapaho chief who had held out
for peace with the white man. After the flight of the
survivors, the Indians rejected Black Kettle and Left
Hand and turned to their war leaders to save them
from extermination.[4]

A Time for Tears

January 14, 1993: I looked around the circle at the inheritors of
this legacy. Some had deep roots in Colorado, both Indian and
European. Some represented families with generations of
involvement with the U.S. Army. All were earnest, humble
believers from towns around the front range. I suggested that
we make confession and ask forgiveness in the presence of the
Lord and our Native American brothers. There were many
tears. Prayers were heartfelt and deeply honest.

One woman stretched herself out in the sand, touching the
feet of an Indian pastor; deeply ashamed she wept for the lost
generation that was cut off in this place. The sense of loss was
upon us all; the beauty of what might have been had these two
peoples walked together in integrity; the generations of alcoholism, suicide and despair that could have been avoided if a culture with the gospel in its roots had exemplified rather than
defamed Jesus to a spiritually hungry people. Minutes turned to
hours as the Spirit of God moved among us. As the day came to
a close we took communion together, and walking in twos we
descended to the sandy streambed where the bodies once lay. I
knelt beside an ancient tree that must have witnessed these events
and poured out the remainder of wine from my communion cup.
I felt sure that people had taken shelter here and died. The red
wine stained the snow where innocent blood was shed. I thanked

Jesus for His innocent blood that takes away the sin of the world.

Wisdom, Patience, Humility

Events like this should not be done quickly. Much thought and prayer preceded the gathering at Sand Creek. Many voices gave their council before any action was taken. The germ of the idea came from an address I gave to the united pastors of the front range many months before at a meeting in Denver. I simply stated that if they wanted revival and harvest they needed to look into the massacre at Sand Creek and the violation of the treaties with the Arapaho and Cheyenne peoples. Perhaps this had never been addressed in a biblical way and was grieving the Spirit of God.

A chapter of the Reconciliation Coalition was formed, including Silas Corea, a godly Indian pastor, and prayer for wisdom began. The first step was the reconciliation ceremony at Confluence Park. The team used great wisdom in communicating invitations, and on the day of the gathering a good representation was present, consisting of government officials from the Colorado Senate and House, the lieutenant governor's office, the Justice Department, the chief of police and the mayor's office.

The northern Arapaho, northern Cheyenne and Kiowa nations sent representatives to participate. Travel expenses and hotel rooms were provided by the coalition team. Also present were young people from the University of Colorado, representing the Hopi, Navajo and Sioux, along with adults from many other tribes who served as witnesses.

Dutch Sheets, a white pastor, began the ceremony with a statement of purpose. I quote in part:

Though we are Christians, we want to state very strongly that we do not believe that this ceremony is the proper occasion to propagate our religious beliefs or to proselytize. We also realize that we do not represent all our invited participants in the statements we make. We state this in the beginning because it is impossible for us to share our purpose or accomplish our goals without mentioning God, and quoting from the Bible.

We believe that our Father God is both grieved and angry over the injustices and the atrocities that we, the white man, have committed against the Native American peoples. We have lied, cheated, stolen, desecrated and killed. These things, apart from the pain and suffering they have visited upon the Indians, also have offended God and aroused His wrath. Isaiah 24:5-6a says, *"The earth is also polluted by its inhabitants, for they transgressed laws, violated statutes, and broke the everlasting covenant. Therefore, a curse devours the earth, and those who live in it are held guilty."*

This description is applicable to us and our relationship with Native Americans.

We are told in Numbers 35:33 that the shedding of innocent blood *"pollutes [and defiles] the land."* We have been guilty of this also. 2 Chronicles 34:21 says, *"For great is the wrath of the Lord which is poured out on us because our fathers have not observed the word of the Lord, to do according to all that is written in this book."* We believe these and other passages teach us that we must assume responsibility not only for our sins, but also for our ancestors. There are numerous examples in the Bible of individuals confessing the shortcomings and transgressions of relatives and predecessors, imploring forgiveness from the Creator as well as the offended parties. This is our purpose for this meeting.

We are commanded by God in Matthew 5:23-24

"If therefore you are presenting your offering at the altar, and there remember that your brother has something against you, leave your offering there before the altar and go your way; first be reconciled to your brother, and then come and present your offering." We believe, on the basis of these and other principles, that God has spoken to us that until we come to the Native Americans for forgiveness and reconciliation even our gifts, to one degree or another, are unacceptable to Him.

We are not naive enough to believe that our words can erase the past or its pain, but we do believe that they can help to shape the future. We come to you in this spirit and for these reasons, we ask for nothing in return but an acceptance of our apology and hopefully an acknowledgement of forgiveness.[5]

After introducing dignitaries, a carefully researched statement was read, itemizing the injustices that had taken place. Then opportunity was given for representatives of various groups to identify with these crimes, express remorse and ask for forgiveness. Many did. The representative from the mayor's office said, "I feel ashamed...on behalf of the mayor and the City Council of Denver I wish to extend my profound apologies for this legacy of lies, theft and death."

Acknowledgment

Confession was made in four categories.

1. **Government — military**

- Dishonest agents of the federal government, in cooperation with railroad, timber, mercantile, and land speculators, defrauded the Indians of their government allotments of land and timber, cash and goods; against which the Native Americans could find no legal recourse.

- The government made and failed to enforce over 300 treaties.
- Although there was a Congressional investigation of the Sand Creek Massacre, the matter was mostly swept under the political rug, and was never satisfactorily resolved.

For the wrongs committed, for the related betrayals of your trust, and for the atrocity of Sand Creek, we offer our apology and ask for forgiveness.

2. Social injustices — prejudices

- Indian peoples have been subjected to numerous social injustices and prejudices. Indian children were removed from their homes in order to make them into "white" children. Sometimes the children were never returned. These children were forbidden to speak their own language in school and were punished for it.
- The Indian people have been subjected to blatant prejudice and subservient positions in society, and we have been insensitive to the problems that confront the American Indian people today such as 90 percent alcoholism, poor health care, lack of adequate housing, alcoholism touching 75 percent of the homes, a suicide rate five times higher than any other ethnic group, excessive high school dropout rates, and an average life-expectancy of only 40.1 years.
- These violations extend even to the graves of your ancestors through the insensitive act of selling the pot-

tery and other articles buried with them and the displaying of bones in museums.

We apologize for these wrongs and injustices, and ask for forgiveness.

3. Sins of those bearing Christ's name

- While seeking to bring Christ to the Native Americans, Christian missionaries sometimes maintained an attitude of superiority and sought to impose a version of the gospel riddled with western cultural forms. In some missions there was economic exploitation of Indian children.
- John Chivington, an ordained Methodist minister who fought hard against slavery during the Civil War, turned a stony heart toward the Native Americans of this land and wantonly slaughtered nonhostile Indians at Sand Creek.

For the destructiveness of zeal without wisdom, and the misguided and insensitive ways in which the Church has dealt with you, we ask your forgiveness.

4. Violation of stewardship of the land

- It has long been accepted and understood among the Indian nations that theirs was a special position in regard to the care of the land. While they did not hold a written title to it, it was understood that the land belonged to all who lived on it, to support life in harmony. By virtue of first right of occupancy, the land was yours for as far as the eye could see.
- Since that time the Indian people have lost the right to

large parts of their land, much of it taken to satisfy the
interests and greed of businessmen and miners, and
most of it in direct defiance of treaty rights, legally established and signed by the government. In other cases,
land speculators made themselves rich buying and selling Indian land from impoverished Native Americans.
This process violated the spirit of Native Americans who
believed they had betrayed a sacred trust in giving up
their God-appointed stewardship of the land.

- White hunters and eastern fur companies were allowed
to wantonly kill off the buffalo herds which were the
mainstay of food, clothing, and shelter for the hunting
tribes of the plains. This forced the Indians, through
starvation, to move into designated reservations. From
1870-1880, thirteen million buffalo were slaughtered.

**For the wrongs committed in the illegal taking of
land, for the government's unwillingness to enforce
legal treaty rights, and for the hundreds of Indian
lives taken in defense of these treaty rights, we ask
for forgiveness.**

Repairing the Breach

The response to this confession was deeply moving. Native
American people are obviously tired of grieving—they want
resolution. John Emhoolah, representing the Kiowa nation,
accepted the church and government apology for the injustice
that was done at Confluence Park: the illegal selling of the
campsite of his great-great-grandfather, Chief Little Raven.
John graciously forgave and said, "Today my prayer has been
answered. We have to love one another and leave things in the
hands of our great Creator." Arnold Hedley, representing the

northern Arapaho from Wind River, Wyoming, said he had forgiven and wanted to see a day when all could live in harmony.

Sylvester Knows-His-Gun, a Cheyenne representative
from Lame Deer, Montana, graciously expressed forgiveness
after stating the enormity of the pain and bitterness that the
Cheyenne had felt over Sand Creek. His statement: "Belatedly,
we welcome you to Indian country. This great land belongs to
all and we welcome you to this country." This was said without
cynicism and had tremendous impact on everyone present.

Theresa Guiterrez, a Cheyenne-Sioux woman, who is
director of American Indian Student Services, spoke with great
honesty, saying, "I think I understand why I am here tonight.
That understanding comes from the fact that I need to heal me,
because I am angry for the suffering my people have had....I
have been suspicious and afraid of white people. I see the racism
every day....I can appreciate the goodness you have in your
hearts for wanting this reconciliation. Maybe what I need to
say is, 'I forgive you.'"

Native American students also expressed themselves. A
Navajo girl, Bo Lewis, thanked the organizers for helping them
face the pain. She said, "We are glad you are standing with us in
this so we can go forward and start the healing."

Perhaps the most encouraging report was that of Andy
Kozad, a Native American who played the drum song for the
Indian color guard. He said that during the ceremony God had
spoken to him and called him into full-time ministry.

Standing in the Gap

The meeting that took place at Sand Creek had various objectives. Believers were the only ones present, and mature intercessors at that. Here we were able to move more overtly in
intercession and spiritual warfare. If anything, the grieving of

the Indians, the remorse of the whites and the healing power of reconciliation was deeper. However, our purpose went beyond these things—it was time to meet with our God. This was a God-anointed prayer meeting involving worship, confession, intercession, proclamation and blessing.

ONE OF THE MOST IMPORTANT THINGS THAT TAKES PLACE IN THE HEART OF OFFENDED PEOPLES AT AN ON-SITE RECONCILIATION CEREMONY IS RELEASE FROM UNRESOLVED GRIEF.

During such times, believers pray as the Holy Spirit leads them and they sometimes participate in prophetic actions. These actions, such as pouring out the communion wine, should never be absolutized, or even taught as a method. They are merely testimonies of how God leads particular groups of people at a particular time. In the Bible we see Jeremiah, in obedience to God, burying his loin cloth down by the river as a prophetic statement. However, we would never teach that all prophets should communicate in this way, let alone build such an action into the liturgy of the Church. (Although I can see that an underwear cult is possible, given the bizarre things that some religious people have emphasized.)

One of the most important things that takes place in the heart of offended peoples at an on-site reconciliation ceremony is release from unresolved grief. On the anniversary of the massacre, a handful of Christians braved the bitter cold and journeyed to Sand Creek. This was several weeks before the larger events I have described. Included in their number was a Native American Christian named Spencer Cody, a dear friend and adviser to me. He describes his experience in his own words.

A vision of the event unfolded (unwanted) as I trudged through the snow. I only saw the children, I only heard their frightened cries. I found a hollow tree and got out of the biting cold wind. I knelt there and asked God "Why? How could any human being kill children in this cowardly manner?" I (surprisingly) blamed no one, I prayed for my children, that this hatred would not find them. I heard children singing in the wind. It was not a song of mourning, it was a song of remembrance. "You have come here, you have remembered us. We have not perished, because you are our blood. Tell your sons and tell your daughters about us, and you shall preserve our memory and we will live yet." I returned to pray with the others. I had released the pain that is healing still. Reconciliation is still possible.[6]

Time for Application

In order to explore your potential as a reconciler, fill in the details alongside the list below:

My gender is:_____

My generation is: _____

My native language is: _____

Subcultures I identify with are: _____

_____

_____

My class (socioeconomic status) would be seen by others as: _____

_____

_____

My religious history has been: _____

My religious affiliation now is: _____

My family name is: _____

List some of the movements, ideologies, and institutions that have touched your family line as far back as you know: _____

_____

_____

My location (region — city — suburb — neighborhood) is:_____

_____

My vocation is: _____

_____

To the people of my extended family I am (i.e., daughter — sister — wife — mother): _____

_____

_____

Referring to the list on pages 117-118, look at what you have written and consider the opportunities for identificational repentance created by your unique identity. It would be nice to just see ourselves as Americans without hyphen — and maybe that day will come — but as long as these wounds remain, believers must use every means within our power to heal the land.

■ ■ ■

Recommended Reading:
Jackson, Helen. *A Century of Dishonor.* New York: Indian Head Books, 1993.

Notes
1.   George Bent to George E. Hyde, April 14, 1906 (Coe Collection, Yale University).

2. U.S. Congress 39th 2nd session, Senate Report 156, pp. 73, 96.
3. Ibid., p. 53, Berthrong, p. 220.
4. Dee Brown, *Bury My Heart at Wounded Knee* (New York: Simon & Schuster, 1970), p. 91.
5. Used by permission.
6. Used by permission from Last Days Ministries, Lindale, Texas.

13

A COSTLY OBEDIENCE

"If anyone wishes to come after Me, let him deny himself, and take up his cross, and follow Me."

Matthew 16:24

Reconciliation is not cheap; it will cost us everything. If we follow Jesus, the Reconciler, we must take up a cross. We must put at risk the things to which we are most deeply attached. We cannot say what this means for the other party, but we must calculate the cost of obedience for ourselves and for our group. Confession is a charade unless it is matched with action. We can call for national days of fasting and repentance, we can weep at a place like Sand Creek and still find the face of God turned from us.

"Why have we fasted and Thou dost not see? Why have we humbled ourselves and Thou dost not notice?" (Isa. 58:3).

God is looking for the depth of our obedience; we must forsake hatred, seek healing between factions and do justice now, regardless of the cost.

> "Is this not the fast which I chose,
> To loosen the bonds of wickedness,
> To undo the bands of the yoke,
> And to let the oppressed go free,
> And break every yoke?
> Is it not to divide your bread with the
>   hungry,
> And bring the homeless poor into the
>   house;
> When you see the naked, to cover
>   him;
> And not to hide yourself from your
>   own flesh?" (Isa. 58:6,7).

Every perceived right and cherished dream must be placed on the altar, including the picture we have of what America should be. Come on, put it there: male privilege; the right to live in a certain place; the right to be surrounded by your own kind, color and language; where everything is dominated by your own architecture and traditions. Put your children on the altar, the expectation that they will marry the same race and bear you grandchildren that look like past generations of family portraiture. What about your possessions? Are they beyond the reach of the restitution that God may require?

Hope for Justice

The day after the meeting at Sand Creek the board of the Native American Affairs chapter of the Reconciliation Coalition met in the home of a Denver oilman. The subject of our discussion was the Wounded Knee Massacre, and we spent hours listening to Indian leaders, including Marrles Moore, a respected Sioux leader from the Rosebud Reservation.

Sitting to one side was our host, a thoughtful man, deeply committed to biblical principles. Late in the evening he walked to a map on the wall and asked if anyone knew the people indigenous to a certain part of Wyoming. The Indian leaders told him; then he stunned us all with a proposal.

> REAL RECONCILIATION INVOLVES TAKING UPON OURSELVES BOTH THE GUILT AND GRANDEUR OF OUR HISTORY AND FACING THE IMPLICATIONS SQUARELY.

"I own the natural gas rights to federal land in that area," the oilman told us. "I pay royalties to the government on every well, but I am prepared to volunteer an additional royalty to the descendants of the Indians displaced by treaty violation from this area."

This was a huge amount of money; we were speechless. I turned to the Indian leaders.

"There are millions of people like him," I said. "They esteem the Word of God above all else and if we can show them that something is biblical, they will obey God to the point of ruthless self-denial. These people represent the greatest hope for justice."

A Particular Obedience

You and I don't know what God may ask of us. We must all live out a particular obedience. What God is looking for in us is an abandonment to His purpose without reservation; a people willing to pay the price for true rather than counterfeit reconciliation. Cheap reconciliation papers over deep-seated differences by suggesting that we can have peace with God, by pretending offenses did not happen or that injustice cannot be addressed. It is a deception to think that all we need is a little good will and decency—that we are one in Christ and existing differences just need to be transcended. This only tempts us to see ourselves reconciled to one another in the spiritual life of the kingdom of God, but not in everyday life. Yes, we need to be born again, but that does not lift us above reality—it empowers us to face it.

It is equally tempting to deny our own identities and attempt to ingratiate ourselves with the other party by constantly fawning on them at the expense of honesty. Real reconciliation involves taking upon ourselves both the guilt and grandeur of our history and facing the implications squarely. We cannot self-righteously denounce our own ancestors and assume the identity of their victims as some college students did during the '60s. This is one of the cheapest and least effective forms of reconciliation.

Who Goes First?

The opposite and equally futile tactic is to place conditions on the other party. "Why should we go first in humbling ourselves? Look at the sins of the other group." This has led to a focus on Indian shamanism or the historic reputation for ruthless cruelty gained by some tribes. "Let the Indians repent of idolatry and then we will be reconciled," is a too-prevalent attitude.

No mention of the sins of Indians was made at Confluence Park or Sand Creek. Nevertheless, I witnessed profound repentance. "We have sometimes worshiped the creature rather than the Creator, forgive us God and restore us to fellowship with You," was one man's prayer. The guiding principle is: "One who knows the right thing to do, and does not do it, to him it is sin" (Jas. 4:17).

Or to put it in our context, if one culture has been blessed with centuries of exposure to God's Word, it will be doubly responsible for its sins and obligated to go first in initiating honest confession and attempts at reconciliation. Missionaries were present among many of the tribes and were often the lone voices speaking out against government policy and settler encroachment, but the fact remains that the Indians were largely ignorant of the gospel in contrast to European-Americans who came from cultures that had been exposed to the gospel of Christ for more than 1,000 years. (If you're Greek or Italian, nearly 2,000 years.)

> GOD WANTS TO GIVE US DEEP AND LASTING GIFTS OF FRIENDSHIP WITH PEOPLE OF OTHER CULTURES. GOD'S STANDARD FOR RELATIONSHIPS IS PURE, FERVENT LOVE, AND THAT TAKES TIME.

We Did That Already

Perhaps the most subtle form of cheap reconciliation would be to overemphasize the significance of solemn assemblies and other formal acts of confession. These ceremonies, though important, are no substitute for confession, repentance, reconciliation and restitution lived out as a way of life. It would be tragic if people prepared spiritual maps and organized ceremonies of identificational repentance at various sites as the latest quick fix, a religious fad that would divert us from commitment to a lifetime of reconciling efforts. God wants to give us deep and lasting gifts of friendship with people of other cultures. After all, His standard for relationship is not, "You don't bother me that much anymore," or, "Stop complaining—we confessed that already." God's standard for relationships is pure, fervent love, and that takes time.

Consider the words of Jesus when the disciples asked Him about the duration of acts of forgiveness: "Seventy times seven" (Matt. 18:22), He told them. In other words, as long as sin and hurt are present in this world, we are never to place limits on the price we will pay to reconcile people to God and to each other. For most of us, the opportunity to be used of God in this way is found in the small affairs of life. This is how it was when Spencer Cody, narrator of the following story, met Sonny Jaynes.

Kiowa Son

I sat looking at the white man sitting a few feet away from me. My heart was cold toward this man and I assumed that he felt the same way about me. It seemed like this was the way it had always been, and the way it would always be. The Indian and the white man as enemies, facing each other in anger and suspicion.

This man, Sonny, had taken me into his home to help me overcome my addiction to alcohol. But Sonny had opened his home to other men who needed help, and now I realized that I had placed myself in the midst of the very thing I hated most: white men. I could have left, but I didn't have any other options in my life at this point.

Things had gone well at first. I kept to myself and just tried to do what was required of me. But then one day we were all out building fences and one of the other men began to antagonize me. Cold fury began to well up within me and before I knew it, I was beating him mercilessly with my fists. He had fallen to the ground, moaning in pain, and I continued to kick him, again and again, until blood was flowing from his face and ears.

I had intended to crush the life from him but, for some reason, I had stopped. Later, when we arrived back at Sonny's house, I still couldn't understand what had stopped me from murdering the other man.

Sonny called me into his office and I thought to myself, *If this white man provokes me, I'm going to hurt him.* He didn't say anything at first, but just sat there looking at me, incredulous at the amount of anger and hatred he had seen pouring out of me.

Sonny kept shaking his head in disbelief, saying, "I just can't understand why you reacted that way!" He paused for a moment and then a look of realization slowly spread across his face.

He blurted out, "Spencer, you have hatred and bitterness in your heart towards all white people!"

I looked at him and said coldly, "Yeah, you're right. And I don't think I like you that much either." I wanted him to react to my words but he did nothing. A few seconds before I had expected Sonny to try and intimidate me as other white men had always done. Instead he had unexpectedly confronted me with the bitterness in my own heart. I felt strangely uneasy.

"Why?" he pleaded. "Why are you so angry?"

In that moment my mind wandered back to my childhood days in Oklahoma...and to my father.

My father was a Kiowa Indian who loved Jesus. As a young man he had been an alcoholic but was miraculously saved on a skid-row street in Los Angeles. He came home to Oklahoma, married my mother and said to himself, "To live in this white man's world, I will need to be like the white man." So he went off to college and got his degree in accounting.

He came back to Oklahoma—but no one would hire him because he was an Indian. He tried and tried to find work but no one would even talk to him. So he took a job as a dishwasher. My father had a college degree, yet he worked in that kitchen washing dishes until he died. My father would always go to church at the Indian mission down the street, but most of the time he'd be the only one there. Preachers to the Indians were few and far between. I remember my father would sit on the front porch of our house in the evenings and sing hymns to Jesus. When I walked by him I was afraid to say a word because the presence of God was all around him. Yet I saw him consistently looked down upon because of the color of his skin.

One particular incident that tore at my heart happened when I was 12 years old. My father and I had been standing in a hardware store for what seemed like an eternity. We had been waiting alone at the counter, but the clerk just continued to ignore us. We waited and waited, but when the door swung open and a few white men came in, the clerk came alive. He greeted them with a warm smile and within a few minutes had taken care of their every need. When the store was once again empty, he turned to my father and his smile disappeared. "Well, what do you want?" he demanded impatiently.

I'll never forget how it felt to see my father humiliated before me. But the painful memories didn't stop there.

My thoughts wandered back to another day that I couldn't forget: the day my sisters and brother and I convinced our parents to let us go with them to town. Our family lived out in the country, so going to town with my parents was a rare treat. It was a big deal for us to be able to play in the park while they went grocery shopping. When they dropped us off at the park and drove away, the four of us were suddenly surrounded by a group of older white children who began to beat us and call us "redskin" and "dirty Indian."

I watched the kids jerk my sister around by her braids as I screamed in frustration, powerless to help her. I watched my baby brother get pushed to the ground while my older sister kept pleading with them to stop slapping her in the face. When at last they left us alone, I cried softly to myself and wondered why being an Indian made us so different.

But all these wounds I hid in my heart.

As I grew older and more bitter, I began to get into fights. I took martial arts classes, and started drinking more and more. There seemed to be no end to the anger inside me. After one particular late night brawl with a bunch of cowboys, I came home, walked inside the front door and heard the unmistakable sound of weeping. I looked down the hall and saw that it was coming from my father. He was praying for me.

When he saw me, he ran and hugged me. Just like the father of the prodigal son, he fell on my neck and wept. Then he looked up to heaven and said, "Thank you, Lord, for bringing my son home safely to me."

All of a sudden I wanted to know this Jesus that could fill a man with such deep love for his family, even in the midst of humiliation and hardship. I had seen a lot of Christian tracts and heard a lot of angry sermons on street corners, but I saw a living example of Christ in my father and I wanted to be like him. So when I was 17 I met Jesus.

I went back to high school with a Bible in my hand. I started preaching and people began to get saved. My father was overjoyed. He came to me and said, "Son, God is going to use you. But if you get a burden, get a burden for the Indian people. The white people have plenty of preachers, but the Indians have nothing."

I looked at him, and it was then I realized I was ashamed of who I was. I had no intention of going to that Indian mission. Instead, my wife and I married right after high school and we started going to a white church. But I felt pressured to change all kinds of things about myself in order to fit in. I was trying to be a young white man and to be successful in the white man's world, but I was living a lie.

I saw my poor father continually going to the mission church and still there were no preachers. I kept trying to live up to the standard of my church, cutting my hair short and wearing all the nice clothes. I got my associate degree from Bible school and started talking the language young preachers talked. But my soul was in deep conflict. I was still attempting to be something I wasn't.

When I was 19 years old and just about to be ordained as a minister, my church split apart. Right then the conflict in my soul reached a breaking point. I laid down my Bible and said to my wife, "I'm not going back. The white folks don't have any more truth than we have."

So for the next two years I walked in rebellion. I drank and became worse. Much worse. I shamed myself and brought reproach upon my family. And right in the middle of that time my father passed away. A couple of months before he died he said to me, "Son, you're breaking my heart. I'm not going to live to see next year, but I have prayed for you. You and all my family will be saved, but I'll not live to see it."

He died soon after that. When we buried him, I looked at his body in that casket and said quietly, without anybody listening, "Dad, I'll see you there." And that's when I turned my heart back to Jesus.

But I still couldn't quit drinking. There was an incredible emptiness inside me, and I was drinking up to a fifth of liquor a day. By this time I was totally addicted. I ended up in the Native American Detoxification Center, but I could only stay there for a few months.

When it was time to leave, I began looking for a rehabilitation program to help me stay sober. I called around and found out about a little ministry in east Texas called "Gates of Life" run by an ex-longshoreman named Sonny Jaynes. I prayed and decided that this was the place to which God was directing me. Little did I know that my long and bitter journey would soon be coming to an end.

■ ■ ■

It seemed like an eternity had passed that day as I looked up at Sonny's face. He was quietly waiting for my answer, his eyes still reflected the question, "Why?"

Waves of pain washed over me as I poured out

memories of my past. I could not hold it back. I just sat there and cried. I cried for my mother, my brothers and my sisters. I cried for my father and I cried for myself.

Then I heard something that I had never heard before. I looked up and Sonny was crying, too. He was crying, and praying. "Lord, forgive us for how we have treated the Indian people. Lord, please forgive us." His head went down and his shoulders were shaking as he wept. My heart began to break as I realized that he was weeping for my people.

"Lord, O Lord, please forgive us."

He looked up at me with tears streaming down his face and said, "Spencer, I can't speak for every white man, but I can speak on behalf of myself and my family. I am sorry for what's been done to the Indian people. Will you forgive me?"

I knew then, deep in my spirit, that Jesus was real. Nobody but a God of love could fill a man with the kind of love and acceptance that was emanating from Sonny at that very moment. Looking up at him, I knew that I would follow Jesus, too.

"For Jesus' sake," I replied. "I forgive you."

Peace flooded my being from that day on. My relationship with Jesus began to take me to a place of deep love for my fellowman. There would come a day when I would look into the eyes of white men and say, "My brothers, I love you."[1]

■ ■ ■

Note

1. Used with permission from Last Days Ministries, Lindale, Texas.

14

WHO ARE
YOU PEOPLE?

The Host People of the Land

The Lord nullifies the counsel of the nations;
He frustrates the plans of the peoples. The counsel of
the Lord stands forever, The plans of His heart from
generation to generation.

Psalm 33:10,11

In some ways the politically correct term "Native American" is unfortunate because the native-born, non-Indian United States citizen may feel diminished by its use. The implication is that if they are not native, they are foreign and don't belong. On the other hand, the term "Indian" has the disadvantage of rising from Columbus's confusion about where he had landed. "Thank God he didn't think he was in Turkey" is the oft-repeated joke among Native peoples.

Indigeneity has become a volatile issue as subcultures search for identity in a changing world. I have heard young Mexican-Americans, the children of recent immigrants, state that they are a conquered people, the rightful inheritors of California, the original possessors of the region. Of course, this is not true in the absolute sense. The Chumash, Pomo, Modoc and other Indian tribes inhabited the California area before the coming of the Spanish and the eventual possession of California by the composite culture of an independent Mexico. Like Americans, Mexicans themselves are a new people, dealing with the complexities of a European culture imposed on an Aztec empire that was built out of the subdued peoples indigenous to Central Mexico.

Even among Native American peoples there is little basis for an absolute claim of "first" status. Several waves of north to south immigration seem to have occurred in the misty past, resulting in distinct linguistic families among Amerindian peoples. In California alone, Hokan, Penutian, Uto-Aztecan, Athapascan, Ritwan, Yukian and Lutuamin languages were spoken. The diverse tribes found by Columbus and Cortez when they first arrived in the New World had immigrants for ancestors who had conquered and displaced earlier peoples.

Indigeneity and Divine Providence

Of course, none of this took God by surprise. In Genesis 10, we see God establishing a division of labor in the human family in which Hamitic peoples (descendants of Noah's son Ham*) began to move outward and pioneer the remote regions of the

*This is a vast simplification made necessary by the constraints of this book. I have included this idea because evolutionists treat the racial types as the casual accumulation of individual variations within the human gene pool. Creationists, on the other hand, see the eight people who survived the flood as carriers of the original God-ordained diversity of the anti-Diluvian cosmos. The four males of the ark could not be the key to race because three were the sons of the fourth, necessarily sharing his racial character. Instead, races were embodied in the four wives, leading biblical scholars to much speculation about the origin of peoples.

earth. The so-called "Age of Discovery," which began 500 years ago, consisted merely of the descendants of Japheth (Indoeuropeans) finally leaving home and taking a look at the planet. What they discovered was that the earth had already been pioneered by Hamitic peoples who, demonstrating a genius for innovation, had produced the technology for survival in every ecological niche from the Arctic wastes to the atolls of the Pacific. It is this understanding of redemptive purpose that gives dignity to Native Americans. I believe they are to be honored as the host people of the land.

As a New Zealander with European ancestry, I have come to see the Maori people in this way. I believe it was divine providence that guided the Polynesian progenitors in their epic sea voyages to New Zealand hundreds of years before the arrival of my European ancestors. The "Tángata whenua" (host people of the land) shaped the foundations of New Zealand's unique personality and the immigrant peoples of the last 200 years have been "adopted" into the Polynesian culture.

I have visited my ancestral homelands of Scotland and England and while I feel a deep bond with the landscape, architecture and language, I am also aware that the people are not my "tribe." I am far closer to my fellow New Zealanders of any race; we are rugged individualists but show evidence of a common "soul." This was first brought home to me when I visited New Zealand after many years overseas. I was teamed with another lecturer at a conference in Auckland. He was a respected Maori Bible teacher named Norman Tawhiao, an elder statesman in the New Zealand church. One afternoon he began to explain Maoritanga (the way of the Maori) to the largely white, middle-class audience. To my surprise, I found that he was describing me. Inside New Zealand it was hard to see, but take a white New Zealander and place him alongside his American, Canadian, Australian and British cousins in an international setting and very distinct differences become apparent.

I made a list of all the New Zealanders I knew well who were missionaries or ministers in other countries, and my suspicions were confirmed. We all exhibited common traits I had never before thought of as Maori. I remember thinking, *I am a white Maori,* as a sense of pleasure enveloped my whole being.

> THE NATIVE-BORN AMERICAN CITIZEN FEELS ROOTED IN THE NORTH AMERICAN LANDSCAPE AND KNOWS NO OTHER HOME. THE SPIRITUAL ATMOSPHERE OF AMERICA HAS SHAPED HIS OR HER SOUL.

This led me to study more carefully the redemptive traits of the indigenous people and for the first time I began to see what God intended for New Zealand. We are not a bit of Europe in the Pacific, nor are we to strive for industrial or military power: we are to give ourselves to the enterprises appropriate to Polynesia. We are to give ourselves to hospitality, healing, food production, entertainment and education; our beautiful land is prophetic, intuitive and comforting at its root.

This same paradox of lost identity surrounds Amerindian and immigrant-descendant relationships in North America. One of the reasons the movie *Dances With Wolves* was such an enormous hit was that many Americans look at Native American culture and subconsciously say, "That's me." The native-born American citizen feels rooted in the North American landscape and knows no other home. The spiritual atmosphere of America has shaped his or her soul.

The other reason *Dances With Wolves* was so popular was that it touched a vast bruise, a storehouse of unresolved white guilt that still weighs down a generation yearning for reconciliation and harmony. This movie was at heart a reconciliation fantasy. The central character is a type of our own generation when he rejects the harsh regimentation of the army and "marries into" the earth—embracing mystic rhythms of Sioux culture.

One of the most destructive forces to enter American culture was the pseudoreligious endorsement given to the Manifest Destiny myth. This myth perpetuated the false idea that the Indians were some kind of pagan "Canaanites" whom God intended to displace in order to give an inheritance to "Israelite" settlers from Christian Europe. This myth does not find its root in the Puritan New England of the 1600s, but rather in the journalists of New York and the politicians of Washington in the 1840s. It is a complete perversion of the Pilgrim's dream.

Let's go back to the beginning. How did the events of 1620 look from God's perspective? I can accept God guiding the Pilgrims to their landing place; however, I also see God guiding the Pemaquid and the Wampanoag Indians with equal purpose.

When the Pilgrims landed in America they were in danger of starvation. They may have carried the gospel to the New World, but they were ill-equipped to survive and needed to be rescued by the Indians. I believe that God fully intended these foundational circumstances to be a parable of mutual respect and dependency, and indeed these Christian Englishmen and their Indian hosts lived in peace for many years. It was not until a less devout generation came to birth that greed for land pushed the Wampanoags into the wilderness and forced a confederacy of tribes to defend themselves from extinction in the War of 1675.

This story of "marriage" or alienation between Indian and European peoples continued to unfold on the eastern seaboard, giving rise to high points, such as the ministry of David Brainerd (a missionary to the Indians of the Sasquehanna Valley), and low points, such as the massacre of the Raritans of Staten Island by Dutch settlers. For 200 years, the love/hate pattern continued as settlers moved through the passes of the Alleghenies and west to the Mississippi and Missouri Rivers, the great wet arteries of the interior. By the 1860s, Christian restraint had almost vanished from race relations and a mad, greedy scramble for the west began in earnest.

> TO OURSELVES, WE ARE ROY ROGERS AND DALE EVANS ON A HAPPY TRAIL; BUT TO THE PEO-PLE OF THE WORLD WE LOOK MORE LIKE A HIGH-PLAINS DRIFTER WITH A FAST GUN AND A SQUINT.

By 1890, the civilization of the American Indian was destroyed and a new myth of American identity was formed, a myth that celebrated audacity and personal freedom above all else and glorified lawless violence. For most, the Indian was reduced to a menacing shadow, subhuman and cruel, fit only for extermination. Unfortunately, this is how much of the world still sees the United States: a cowboy culture with a smoking gun and an arrogant sneer; a fragmented people rich in booty but racked by violence. The ugly American. To ourselves, we are Roy Rogers and Dale Evans on a happy trail; but to the peoples of the world we look more like a high-plains drifter with a fast gun and a squint.

Reconciliation with Native Americans is foundational. There is a hindrance to God's blessing on this nation as long as this wound remains unhealed. Without the embrace and blessing of the "host" people, Americans will fall short of apprehending both their identity and destiny. Let's face it: The only culture that's truly unique to the United States is that of the indigenous peoples. The rest of us can only contribute a modified version of a transplanted African, Asian or European root.

I believe there is to be much more than reconciliation and peaceful coexistence with justice. I believe there is to be a flowering of Indian decorative arts, language, culture and dance that is championed by the Church.* For too long, charismatic and Pentecostal Christians have associated anything Indian with the demonic. It would be tragic if some of the most earnest, committed Christians inflicted the deepest wounds of rejection upon Indians simply because they did not understand the difference between form and meaning in culture. As a missionary, I understand the tragic insensitivity and ignorance of some of my predecessors and I cling to the example of the first missionary to Europe, the apostle Paul.

Paul and the Pagans

When Paul ascended Mars Hill, he was confronted by the idolatry and superstition of Greek culture. He was surrounded by things worthy of denunciation. He could have launched into a prophetic tirade, but he did not. Instead, he fixed on the altar to the unknown god and began to magnify the revelation of the Creator, already present within Greek history.

To speak of all the redemptive analogies present within the traditions of the indigenous peoples of North America would take several more books. It is sufficient to say they are there— God has not left Himself without a witness. We need to learn before we presume to teach. In short, we need to return to the mutual dependency that God established when the Pilgrims first stepped onto these shores and met Samoset, Massasoit, Squanto and Hobomah.

The deep spirituality within the Indians, if truly awakened in right relationship with God, will lead to reconciliation with

---

*In the traditional Navajo marriage ceremony, white cornmeal, representing the woman's family, is mixed with the male family's yellow cornmeal, symbolizing two lives combined into one. This is just one example of a traditional form with a redemptive meaning. Obviously, nothing is intrinsically evil about such a practice. It is just a form of communication that is non-European. Every people should be free to express biblical values in their own way, just as they have a right to study God's Word in their own language.

one another, a place of leadership within American Christianity and a radical contribution to world missions. The one thing that could thwart this potential is a repeat of the cycle of rejection and injustice within this generation.

The greatest danger we face is that the politically correct education our children are now receiving will burden young whites with unresolved guilt, inadvertently radicalizing them into defensive prejudices that will only deepen the divide. Better to be ignorant of history than to loose its dark secrets on a culture ill equipped for resolution.

My son David (16 at the time), upon watching the story of Chief Joseph and the Nez Percé on television, turned to my wife with the comment, "I hate being white."

In the nurture of family discussion he was soon able to explore the issue and channel his feelings wisely, without self-hatred. But what about the kid whose dad is not writing a book on the subject? And what about the biggest issue of all, the fact that we whites once enslaved millions of people, justifying it only by the color of their skin?

■ ■ ■

15

WHITE GUILT, BLACK ANGER

For he himself is our peace, who has made the two one and has destroyed the barrier, the dividing wall of hostility.

Ephesians 2:14 (*NIV*)

She wakes up in a cold sweat, haunted by the same nightmare: a necklace of burning tires is searing her flesh, all around her people are cheering.

The daylight reveals a comfortable home; the dream, a collage of images from television. White, Afrikaans-speaking writer Natasha Mostert begins another day.

During breakfast she watches the news. On this day it is different. The surreal pictures of burning palm trees and rioting are not from her own South Africa but from Los Angeles, in the land of the free. She smiles at the snide remark made by the local broadcaster that South Africa should consider imposing sanctions against the United States. It is good to feel good about being South African for a change, but the facts outside her door begin to press in. A black policeman has been killed and mutilated by other blacks, a white man has murdered a black taxi driver for "target practice." Both crimes are defended by some as the acts of people enraged beyond endurance. Natasha, full of emotion, turns to her craft. In *Newsweek*, October 5, 1992, she writes:

> I, too, am angry. As a white, Afrikaans-speaking South African, I realize that I am not entitled to this anger. After all, I belong to an ethnic group that has caused misery to the majority of people with whom it shares the land.
>
> I envy my friends in the United States and in Europe, their guilt-free existence: their certainty that they are entitled to build careers, make homes, better their lives. I wonder what it must be like to live your life without the thought scratching at the back of your mind that you are not really allowed—that you are building with tainted tools, that the foundation of your life rests on the sins of the fathers; that you should make amends.[1]

If only it was so. Natasha has forgotten that not too long ago slavery was practiced in America. We do not live the guilt-free existence she imagines. In the long view of history, our legacy may be worse.

Indeed, America's loud condemnation of South Africa is precisely because of our own racist legacy. Like the sinner who sees his own sin reflected in the actions of others, we shout denunciation of South African policy in the hope that it will drown the voice of our own troubled conscience.

"We Didn't Sell Them into Slavery"

Today's American high school students are profoundly aware of the dark side of the American story and they are reacting to it with strong opinions. *Los Angeles Times* reporter, Rogena Schuyler, recently displayed her collection of essays on the subject, all written by white students:

Janna from Hacienda Heights, California, writes:

I don't think white people owe anything to black people. We didn't sell them into slavery, it was our ancestors. What they did was wrong, but we've done our best to make up for it.

Matthew from Diamond Bar, California, says:

Slavery is a part of America's past that cannot be erased or forgotten...there have been those over the years who have recognized injustice and sought to do something about it...however, once again we find history repeating itself...man harbors a prejudice in his heart that is passed from generation to generation. Until we can keep what is in the past in the past and focus on the future, we are doomed to repeat history.

Perhaps most typical is the reaction of Deanna who attends high school in Los Angeles proper. She is angry about the whole thing.

I'm not safe from persecution in the classroom. I feel we spend more time in my history class talking about what whites owe blacks than just about anything else. When the issue of slavery comes up I often receive dirty looks. This seems strange given that I wasn't even alive then. And the few members of my family from that time didn't have the luxury of owning much, let alone slaves. So why, I ask you, am I constantly made to feel guilty? Even though some of my best friends have been black and are not prejudiced, they do not represent the vast majority of African-Americans in L.A. who are increasingly leaning toward hatred of non-blacks.

Why is it OK for them to preach against whites, Asians, Latinos, whoever? Why am I the butt of racist jokes, and why isn't anyone else speaking out? Why is it OK for blacks to forget common courtesy when in contact with me? And why am I expected to put up with it?

I'm so tired of anything and everything being turned into a racial issue. I'm tired of people looking at my skin and not only judging me, but thinking I owe them something. What's wrong with looking and acting "white" (whatever that is)? Can't I have pride in my Irish-Hungarian ethnicity?[2]

Like millions of other white Americans, Deanna is experiencing the daily reality of black anger; she is struggling with rejection and beginning to express resentment.

Chains in the Promised Land

When a people have been oppressed and wounded and the yoke is lifted, when the circumstances finally change, the emancipation of their souls is not immediate. The first generation, those who are free but carrying the memory of hurt, are often too numb to be angry. We will call them the survivors; they are shell shocked by life and quietly struggling to build some foundation of normalcy. The past is literally unspeakable, and like veterans who have seen the horrors of war, they are reluctant to talk about it. Their goal is to shield their children from what has hurt them—to put the past as far behind them as possible. They want security, comfort and a future for their children.

This means that the second generation, the children of survivors, are often relatively ignorant of the suffering that overshadows the recent past. It is often the third generation that stumbles across the awful truth in their search for understanding about identity: the unspeakable is spoken about and anger and bitterness surface into the public domain. This also means that the grandchildren of the oppressor often face the greatest hostility and rejection from elements of the offended people group, leaving them bewildered and struggling for an appropriate response.

> I WOULD MUCH RATHER SEE ANGER AND DEFIANCE THAN THE HOPELESSNESS OF A CRUSHED SPIRIT. ANGER IS ENERGETIC; IT CAN BE GIVEN PURPOSE AND CHANNELED TO CONSTRUCTIVE ENDS.

Of course, the human story is less tidy than this model suggests. American slavery lasted for more than 250 years and segregation lingered into this century. This is much longer and more severe than the traumas experienced by most peoples. The Civil War took place 130 years ago, yet only now is a tone of defiance and anger coloring the search for a black identity. The "in your face" attitude that characterizes the rapper, the activist and the gangster has other causes—particularly the personal pain of family disintegration. However, reaction to the legacy of slavery is a factor. After all, it was not until the 1970s that the miniseries "Roots" was shown on national television and the personal experiences of African-American slaves began to be fully appreciated by both black and white Americans.

I see black anger as a sign of hope. It is frightening to me personally as a white man living in the black community, but I would much rather see anger and defiance than the hopelessness of a crushed spirit. Better the warrior with a cause than the hollow-eyed addict or the fawning servility of a people without an identity. Anger is energetic; it can be given purpose and channeled to constructive ends. Angry people often search for answers. The good news is that there are potential prophets of justice and reconciliation among today's black children. Martin Luther King Jr. was not the first black reconciler and he will not be the last. The question is: How will the rest of society respond to their message? This brings us to the issue of white guilt.

> WHILE PERSONAL GUILT IS DAILY MINIMIZED BY THE GURUS OF PSYCHOBABBLE, CORPORATE GUILT HAS NEVER BEEN MORE POPULAR AS A CONCEPT.

Who, Me?

Oliver Stone, the moviemaker, was recently asked whether in the wake of the Los Angeles riots he feels lucky or guilty about his own good fortune. He answered without pause, "No, I don't feel guilty—that's a Western Christian trip."[3]

We live in a day in which the self-help movement has sought to eradicate guilt by defining it as psychologically damaging. Remorse is out of fashion. Nobody is guilty. We need to learn to love ourselves, to forgive ourselves; we are never guilty, just pathetic, the experts say. It has become increasingly fashionable to blame guilty feelings on Christianity, as though these dark feelings are a condition of inculturation rather than something arising from the fundamental nature of human beings. In reality, the problem is not that there is too much guilt, but too little; not the unmoored guilt of ambiguous Freudian anxiety, but the real thing, a robust moral guilt that tells us when we have transgressed.

While personal guilt is daily minimized by the gurus of psychobabble, corporate guilt has never been more popular as a concept. Redress of grievance is one of the great rationales of our day, often given as the justification for government programs, laws, curriculum changes and what the black author, Shelby Steeles, calls "grievance identities."[4] White children raised in the '90s are increasingly bombarded with the accusations of offended subcultures, the most notable example so far being the huge following gained by angry Afrocentric rappers among white teenage boys.

Most people understand that race should not be a source of advantage or disadvantage in a free society, and whites in America generally know there is at least a slight advantage in being white. This kind of knowledge makes them uneasy, but it is the long shadow of history that makes them truly vulnerable. At any moment they may hear, "Hey Whitey, you oppressor of my people, all that you have is tainted, built on centuries of advantage."

The power to inflict shame is an enormous power, and eventually a group of defense mechanisms emerges among those trying to shield themselves from accusation.

In order to see how a people group responds to the weight of corporate guilt, we will lift our discussion outside the American context for a moment.

Born Guilty?

The most dramatic story of this century is the rise and fall of the Third Reich, a global catastrophe that bequeathed to today's

Germans a legacy of shame almost without precedent in the human experience.

Recently, an alarming resurgence of neo-Nazism and right-wing extremism is occurring in Germany. But at the same time, hundreds of thousands of people all over the country have demonstrated against the neo-Nazis in support of democracy, foreigners and tolerance. When asked to explain this, Germany's foremost pollster, Elisabeth Noelle-Neumann, reveals that the extremists are not representative of the culture as a whole and that they fall into two categories: one on the left and one on the right. Most interestingly, she has discovered that most neo-Nazis are young people between the ages of 14 and 19 and that the left-wing extremists are a lot older—usually between 20 and 30. This age disparity demonstrates the ricochet effect of corporate guilt as it is handed off like a hot potato from one generation to another. Noelle-Neumann traces this reaction back to the Nazi period when Hitler and his associates exploited the qualities, abilities and ideals of the German people in order to satisfy their craving for power.[5]

During the writing of this book, I spoke to a large number of German Christian leaders gathered at Lüdenscheid in the Ruhr. The subject of our conference was, "Gottes Berufung Für Deine Nation" (God's Calling for Our Nation). During this time, I came across the work of Peter Sichrovsky, an Austrian Jew, who had compiled into a book a series of interviews with the children and grandchildren of committed Nazis, most of them involved in running the death camps. The title of his book? *Born Guilty.*[6]

Sichrovsky's interviews are a classic study of the enormous impact of unresolved corporate guilt on successive generations. Here is a sample of the intense reactions he discovered. It is obvious that the army of psychologists who labored during the 1960s and 1970s were unable to move their charges from the memory of collective barbarism to collective amnesia and happy serenity.

Anna: "We invited neither his parents nor mine to our wedding. That was the worst thing we could do to them. For days my mother cried, and his father threatened to disinherit him. But we didn't want them around. We wanted to make a fresh start. No witness from the past."

Rudolf: "I must tell you that I am haunted by guilt....Guilt now rests upon my shoulders. My parents, they're already roasting in hell. They died a long time ago; it's over for them, this life. But they left me behind. Born in guilt, left behind in guilt....Just look at me. Innocent, I am living the life of a guilty person...I must not have children. This line must come to an end with me...I lived with my parents too long, who knows what evil I carry within me? It mustn't be handed down."

Johannes: "How lovely it would be, a life without a past. Sometimes I wish that both of them had died when I was small."

Rainer: "Yes, I am waging war on the German past. I long for the day when the last survivor of the Third Reich will be dead. I look forward to their extinction. Perhaps then we'll finally get a chance for a new Germany."

Brigitte: (Rainer's sister; in response) "You're not the new wonderful breed you think you are. Your left-wing enthusiasm was nothing but spite against Father. Just think how you decorated your room. Ridiculous! A Mao portrait here, a Lenin picture there, a Marx bust on the desk. Later the Star of David on a neck chain, and after that a Palestinian shawl draped over your shoulders. What other disguises do you still need? Do you want me to go on? Just look at yourself!"

Susanne: "Well, yes basically what I did was to ask my son for forgiveness and, beyond that, for an appreciation of my situation. I left no doubt about my own rejection of the past and my father's deeds....I forged a bond with my son—against my own father."

Monika: "...but I refuse to see things in terms of black and white. I always try to see both good and bad in people....I studied psychology and after graduating got a job in a prison working on an experimental program of alternative approaches to punishment."

Igon: "Once we had to write a composition on the topic 'The Role of the Medical Profession in the Crimes of National Socialism.'...I wrote a paper defending the doctors, using the arguments I'd heard from my father...soon after entering medical school, I joined a student group, dedicated to the protection of Germanhood....As I have already told you, I would have acted the same way. I can imagine that this disturbs you. But I'm not going to stand here as a man who denies his father. On the contrary, I'm proud of him....I will do things differently, yet without being different."

Ingeborg: "I got very interested in Jews. I developed a sort of reverse prejudice....I identified with the victims....Perhaps my life here in Austria with a Jew is also my personal contribution to reconciliation and restitution."

Stefan: "I am not responsible for what my father did. I wasn't born then and I have nothing to do with it....I think of myself as being in the other camp, someone who is suffering under him, just as all those others during the Third Reich."

Werner: "I suddenly became aware of the possibility that my father's deed could also be part of me, even though I wasn't even born at the time....I devote all my energy to teaching: Seminars on fascism, lectures about the resistance movement, excursions to concentration camps, and so on."

Sichrovsky points out that in the 50 years since the war the problems facing young Germans have changed radically. Those who came of age during the postwar period were told next to nothing about the Nazi era, while today's youth complain that all they hear is that they were, and perhaps still are, a nation of murderers and accomplices. He concludes that both defensive and accepting reactions indicate that young Germans are preoccupied with the past. Indifference is rare. Even in the fourth generation, it seems that time does not heal these wounds.

Guilt and Prejudice

In the words of these tormented young Germans we hear an exaggerated version of the reactions to corporate guilt found in every nation. Reading of their efforts fills me with sadness because not one experienced true cleansing. Even Ingeborg, who married a Jew and sounds the most hopeful, finally concludes:

> What I've gotten is inner turmoil, being torn out of my setting without finding a new one.

The most frightening reaction is the defiant position taken by Igon, who justifies his father's actions by vilifying the Jews. He said:

> The system failed. Not in its ideas, but in its execution. Well, maybe in some of its ideas, but not in the

basic ones. I always spoke up when I heard the Nazi
era being indiscriminately attacked.

It is the voice of Igon that grows loudest in the 1990s, not
just in the words of easily vilified Serbian politicians, but also in
the quiet hardening of attitudes here in America.

Unresolved corporate guilt is an invisible force moving
each generation toward polarization. Nobody is free from reaction. What have you chosen? These are some of the options I
have seen people choose.

1. Submerging themselves in the aggrieved culture.
2. Taking on the identity of a victim and wallowing in
   self-pity.
3. Practicing denial about the whole thing.
4. Adopting the opposite ideology or religion from their
   roots in the hope that that will help.
5. Retreating into a world of deterministic philosophy
   where biology explains everything and guilt is deemed
   inappropriate.
6. Rejecting their national or racial identity by moving
   abroad, becoming an "enlightened" world citizen.
7. Loudly denouncing their own ancestors.
8. Claiming to be part of a unique category that never
   had anything to do with it.
9. Retreating into a separate community and pretending that the aggrieved culture does not exist.
10. Defiantly defending their ancestors and vilifying their
    victims.

Outwardly, almost everybody chooses a combination of
the first 9 options, but inwardly we choose option number 10.

Don't be fooled. We all carry prejudice and the first step in overcoming it is to admit that we do.

■ ■ ■

It was the 1980s. I was vegging out in my home in Los Angeles, watching TV. The next news item was about a commemorative civil rights march in which aging activists and supporters were retracing a march route through the South in celebration of the victories of the 1960s. The whole thing was turning into a night- mare. As they left the outer suburbs of a large city, they encoun- tered unexpected resistance in the affluent semirural counties to the north. The roads were lined with angry faces, the air thick with racial aspersions and threats. I could hardly believe it. What year was this? Do people still do this stuff?

A few months later I found myself ministering in that exact area. I noticed the complete absence of black people. It was a white wilderness. These people were not basing their prejudice on experience; these attitudes were inherited. They are part of the ethos of a people group, passed down from parent to child in a thousand small ways in each generation. In their insulated enclave, these people never related to African-Americans. They did not have the opportunity to be either hurt or helped by blacks. Their hatred and anger seems completely irrational until we look beneath the surface and see unresolved corporate guilt, the main contributor to antiblack prejudice among white Americans.

Let's personalize it.

What if you and I were two hippies living near the Rogue River in the 1970s? My commune is back in the woods and yours is down by the river. At our place we run out of dope and I'm assigned to make a trip to Portland in order to score a new supply. I swim the river, sneak into your camp and steal your Volkswagen van. Within hours, I have made my connection and am on my way back home, but I have begun to like the idea of having wheels. Instead of ditching the van I divert it to a friend's garage, spray white paint over your psychedelic paint job and then take it back to my place on the Rogue. I am never caught.

Life goes on until we both get saved in the Jesus Movement of 1972-1973. We end up in the same Calvary Chapel. I'm never comfortable around you. Every time I see you I go the other way. I tell myself, "That van is long gone. I can't give it back, I did that before I got saved. It's under the blood; Jesus forgave me. I'll just forget about it." But I can't forget about it. Escape from the past is not so easy. Tension remains between you and me and my conscience continues to bother me. I decide that I'm under condemnation from the devil and I renounce it, but my heart only becomes more troubled as the years go by. I find you increasingly intolerable; I don't even want to look at you. I begin to detest many things about you. I move to another church.

We're now both in our 70s. Life is drawing to a close. Because of the weight of an approaching eternity and the relentless prodding of the Holy Spirit, I finally search for you. I am awkward and embarrassed, but I blurt out my story. You can barely remember that old van, but it solves the mystery of why I treated you so badly. I experience an in-rush of the peace of God. My communion with God is unhindered for the first time.

I hope you see in this parable the dynamic of transference: the human tendency to justify our actions by placing blame on the victims of our crimes. This has gone on long enough in black/white relations.

Our story reaches a resolution because the principles became Christians and the Holy Spirit pursued the guilty one until cleansing and reconciliation took place. The pagans can do very little about deepening prejudice, but the followers of Jesus have the potential to heal the wound. This is our only hope. Without hope, our hearts just turn to stone.

■ ■ ■

Notes

1. Natasha Mostert, "My Turn," *Newsweek*, October 5, 1992.
2. Compiled by Rogena D. Schuyler, *Los Angeles Times*.
3. Interview in *American Way* magazine, 1993.
4. Shelby Steele, "The New Segregation," *Imprints* magazine, August 1992. Vol. XXI. Hillsdale, MI.
5. Interview, Thomas Quinn and Stefanie Heib in *Lufthansa Bordbuch*, February 1993.
6. Peter Sichrovsky, *Born Guilty: Children of Nazi Families* (New York: Basic Books, Inc.), pp. 17-138.

16

REMOVING THE STAINS OF SLAVERY

No Task Is Too Big for Jesus

*And the God of peace will soon
crush Satan under your feet.*

Romans 16:20

Springtime is pleasant in Los Angeles. My spade slices the moist earth and turns the garden soil in the sunlight. Tract houses, separated by redwood fences, sprawl across the valley and lap against the brown hills; this house is mine and I enjoy it.

I hear voices in the background. Suburban sounds; yard work, children at play, the bump-bump of a basketball in a driveway.

"I reject Jesus!" A door slams. "I reject Christianity! That's the religion of the slave owner!" The angry words tumble over the fences and strike at me like a teamster's whip.

"Don't put that on God," comes a female voice in reply. "Jesus didn't do that to us!"

I put down my shovel and listen to the exchange with grief and embarrassment. A Christian woman is defending God's character with all her heart, but the young man's voice is bitter and decided.

I realize her disadvantage. As an African-American, she cannot say certain words, words a young black man should hear. I look down at white man's hands and forearms and seize my opportunity.

Walking through the house and up the street, I begin to search for the house exuding the angry words, rehearsing my confession:

"Excuse me, I couldn't help but overhear what you said. My name is John, I live nearby. I just want to say that I am ashamed of what people of my race did to people of your race. Many of us knew Jesus then but completely misrepresented Him. God is not like a slave owner, He is like a father. I just want to say that I deeply regret these things and ask for your forgiveness. Slavery should never have happened; it broke God's heart. You should not go through life without hearing these words, even if you hear them only once, from a stranger. Please forgive us."

I think of that Saturday with disappointment. I remember pausing before several houses, listening, but the silence had returned. I never did find the right house. I walked back home in sadness. Jesus should be seen as He is.

But there have been other times, many of them.

Perhaps the most poignant time was when a Los Angeles radio station called me during the heat of the riots in April 1992. The interviewer had just three questions.

"Are you safe? Is there still hope? Could you do your repentance thing, now, on the air?"

What better time? I thought, and began to broadcast my halting confession into that terrible night.

Cotton Country

The year is 1831. Old-timers spit tobacco and watch pigs root-ing down Main Street from the shade of the courthouse. Set in rolling forested hills, surrounded by plantations, this smoky cluster of buildings is the county seat.

The road leaves town, passing a plantation boasting a two-story house with columned front porches and a line of out-buildings. Down behind the last barn are the cabins, home to 145 African slaves. Only two other plantations harbor such wealth; these three families are the aristocrats of the county.

One-third of the white families own no slaves and the majority who do own no more than 10. They cannot afford overseers and must work alongside their Negroes in the orchards and cotton patches. The outlying crossroads towns each serve a cluster of charmless farms, supporting small, two-story "big houses" surrounded by various satellite sheds, a one-room kitchen and a barn. Out in back are the slave quarters, built close to the pungent outhouses, convenient to the fields. A menagerie of horses, mules, cows, hogs, dogs and chickens share the compound. Close by stand a few fruit trees, beyond which lie the haystacks and corn and cotton patches.

It is the Lord's Day in Virginia. The town is as full as it gets. Sundays are for preaching and picnics. White folks like to get together after church for a barbecue, cheer on a horse race or just get drunk, joke and gossip. People feel good about themselves. By southern standards, theirs is a culture of enlight-ened benevolence. Why, slavery is never as harsh in Virginia as it is on the brutal cotton plantations of the *deep* South. An occasional white man who hankers after slave girls perhaps, or a sadistic overseer or two, but nothing like the brutality found in Georgia or Mississippi. Virginians like to think all is sweetness and light in their master-slave relations.

The best proof of this is seen on Sundays. Respectable Virginians even take their slaves to white churches and let them sit in the back. Seems to convert them, too. Why, after church they gather in a field or shed for their own praise meetings, although they make such noise with their "gabble."

Bartholomew, the slave, sees things differently. His bright capable mind early acquired the skill of reading and his knowledge of the Bible is prodigious. He sees through the carefully rehearsed teachings given by Master Vincent; portions of the Bible misquoted to keep slaves in humble submission. For every passage white preachers use to vindicate slavery, Bartholomew sees an opposite injunction against human bondage. He knows what the Bible says and has his own ideas about it, but to understand is to know even greater pain:

• To see his wife — poor enslaved child — ordered and pushed around over at Jackson's place, a victim of white peoples' every whim. Even the polygamy of his African forebears was better than this. At least it kept them together.

• To toil and die like cattle (however affectionately treated) in this hypocritical Christian society where white people gloried in the teachings of Jesus and yet completely shunned the "free coloreds" and kept all the other blacks in chains.

• Where slave masters boasted of their Christian charity ("in Virginia we take care of our 'niggers'") and yet broke up families.

Bartholomew knew that at any time he could be sold off to whip-happy slave traders if money was scarce. How could he father his children? He would be just a visitor without legal or recognized status. It meant nothing to snatch a man away and sell him elsewhere. How could he remain loyal when he was expected to "take up" with some new woman on this new plantation, while his dear wife was expected to "breed" with a new man back at Jackson's? Would they both now produce "property" for the master? Precious little ones who would spend their days in ceaseless drudgery without hope?

Why was a proud, godly man with black skin denied something even the most debauched and useless poor white man enjoyed: his freedom?

I Once Was Blind

There was a time when slavery was practiced by nearly every people group. Emancipation is a modern phenomenon that arose as a consequence of the evangelical revival of the mid-eighteenth century in England, which was itself derived from the preaching of John Wesley.

Two thousand years before Christ, slavery was an unquestioned fact of everyday life. Under regimes such as that of Hammurabi, the great Babylonian king, slaves were not even considered as human beings before the law but as livestock. However, the thread of truth running back to righteous Noah was not completely broken. The book of Job, the oldest in the Bible, condemns the inequality that separates master and slave: "If I have despised the cause of my manservant or my maidservant when they complained against me, what then shall I do when God rises up? When He punishes, how shall I answer Him? Did not He who made me in the womb make them? Did not the same One fashion us in the womb?" (Job 31:13-15, *NKJV*).

The Greeks were no more enlightened than the Egyptians or Babylonians. A master could punish his slave in any way he thought fit, short of actually killing him, and some slaves were even obliged to undergo torture on their master's behalf in order to pay for a crime.

By 146 B.C., the Romans were the masters of the civilized world and slavery reached vast dimensions as conquered peoples were forced to labor in chains in quarries and agricultural estates throughout Italy and Sicily. Repression of slave revolts was brutal. Crucifixion* was invented as a special form of death reserved for slaves; its purpose was to impose such degradation and pain that all slaves would tremble in subservience. After Spartacus's uprising in the first century B.C., 6,000 rebels were crucified along the Appian Way.

Slavery continued in Italy even as Christianity ascended in importance, but began to be addressed by Christian leaders such as Pope Gregory. He founded the mission to the Anglo-Saxons, which was headed by St. Augustine after he saw slave boys from Britain in a Roman market. The growing influence of Christianity touched many beyond the Church. Hadrian abolished a master's power of life or death over his slaves, and the nominal Christian emperor Justinian allowed slaves who entered a monastery to become freemen and punished to death those found guilty of raping a slave woman.

After the collapse of Rome, slavery in Europe waned, not undergoing significant revival until the eighth to tenth centuries. This is when Germans captured hoards of Slavs, thus contributing the word "slave" to the Germanic languages, including modern English.

The greatest expansion of slavery took place in the mid-seventh century when Islam spread south from Arabia to Egypt and across the western desert to Tunisia, Lybia and Morocco. The Berbers, native to the area, had already probed as far as Ghana in search of trade goods and slaves. Sub-Saharan Africa was soon traversed with great merchant camel caravans that carried black slaves from as far as Lake Chad in the south to the Arab ports on the Mediterranean. Arab geographer, Al-Yaqubi, wrote in the ninth century, "I have been informed that the kings of the blacks sell their own people without justification or in consequence of war."

Slave-based societies rose and fell for hundreds of years in

---

*In His death by crucifixion, Jesus totally identified Himself with the slaves of all history.

Africa, including the city-states of Hausaland, where slaves lived in a circle of villages beyond the city walls, existing only to produce food for the populace within. The great Mandingo Empire of what is now Mali gave way to the Songhay and, along with the coastal states of the Guinea forest, stood ready to profit by joining their slaving traditions with the European Atlantic trade. In the fifteenth century, the Portuguese approached the coast of Africa.

Prince Henry had an ambitious plan to outflank the Muslims by establishing himself on the south coast. Two of his captains, instructed to bring back anything of value, captured 12 men, women and children as booty. The Pope, enthusiastic about anything that would blunt the power of the Moors, granted complete forgiveness of sins to anybody who would engage in war against them. The Arab monopoly of Trans-Saharan traffic in slaves was finally broken when horses, silk and silver were traded to the rulers of Mali and Songhay in return for nearly 1,000 slaves.

In 1481, the Portuguese were permitted to build a fort at Elmira on the Gold Coast. The terrible years of the Atlantic slave trade had truly begun.

The institution of African slavery moved from the Old World to the New World as an inevitable result of Columbus's discovery. By the time he set foot in the West Indies, black slaves were being imported into Europe at the rate of more than 1,000 a year.

Of course, slavery was not new to the Americas. If anything, the brutality practiced by its ancient conquering empires and small raiding tribes surpassed that of other places. The Spanish conquest continued in the same tradition, until forced labor along with European diseases had so decimated the Amerindian population that an alternative source of cheap labor had to be found. In 1537, Charles V, the deeply religious young emperor, granted the right to ship 4,000 Africans a year to Hispaniola, Cuba, Jamaica and Puerto Rico.

The Portuguese-Spanish monopoly was soon challenged by the energetic maritime nations of northern Europe; first the Dutch, then the French, Danes, Swedes, Germans and then the English. The signing of the treaty of Utrecht in 1713 resulted in the coveted Asiento, an edict giving the English the right to introduce 144,000 black slaves into the Spanish colonies over a period of 30 years.

The surging demand for cane sugar—a crop originally from India—initially drove the slave ships across the Atlantic. In order to sustain the prosperity of the New World, Africans were imported at the rate of 100,000 a year. They were not the only source of labor for the Caribbean and American colonies: white indentured servants were subject to even greater degradation.

In theory, the system of indenture sounded fair, but in practice it led to violent abuses. Less valuable a commodity than the black, who was a slave for life and who produced children of the same status, a master had no incentive to keep his white indentured servant alive for longer than the period of his contract. One French historian wrote, "I knew one 'master' at Guadeloupe who buried more than 50 upon his plantation whom he had killed by hard work and neglect when they were sick. The cruelty proceeded from their having them for three years only, which made them spare the Negro rather than these poor creatures."[1]

However, the enslavement of Africans had an insidious spiritual and social dimension that undermines the identity and worth of Afro-Americans to this day.

The Erasure of Identity

Unlike other minorities within the United States, blacks have been cut off from their cultural roots and subjected to unrelenting and methodical discrimination, sporadically reinforced with violence. How was this treatment justified by a Christian civilization?

Biologically, there are no races. So-called racial characteristics vary so much from individual to individual that all attempts at establishing distinct biological units that deserve classification are arbitrary. Each person has tens of thousands of different genes. At the genetic level, human beings are incredibly diverse in a way that transcends geographic dispersion. Therefore, what we call a race is a classification of culture, having more to do with tribal membership or national citizenship than any real genetic distinction.

AT THE GENETIC LEVEL, HUMAN BEINGS ARE INCREDIBLY DIVERSE IN A WAY THAT TRANSCENDS GEOGRAPHIC DISPERSION. WHAT WE CALL A RACE IS A CLASSIFICATION OF CULTURE, HAVING MORE TO DO WITH TRIBAL MEMBERSHIP OR NATIONAL CITIZENSHIP THAN ANY REAL GENETIC DISTINCTION.

For some reason, skin color has been the defining characteristic in cross-cultural relationships. No personal physical feature, except gender, has made such an impact on the fates of individuals and people groups, yet pigmentation is a relatively superficial thing.

This tendency to classify by color took on its most sinister overtone in the Americas. In ancient societies, slaves were not always drawn from a different racial group than their masters and few questions were raised regarding their basic humanity.

When people from the civilization of Western Christianity became involved in the slave trade, they were immediately presented with a theological problem, namely that the first obligation of a faithful Christian was to convert people and serve them in love, not kidnap them or own them like a beast.

It became necessary, therefore, to dehumanize those people Europeans held in bondage, and shortly before 1700 a proliferation of theories arose about the inferiority of Negroes. If the black African or the Carob Indian was seen as fully human, possessing an immortal soul subject to the potential of salvation, an irreconcilable contradiction arose between the Christian message and chattel slavery.

These dehumanizing arguments were not unchallenged by Christian leaders. Pope Paul III (1534-1549) proclaimed as the work of the devil "the opinion that the inhabitants of the West Indies...should be treated like animals that have no reason."

In modern times, the theological debate gave way to scientific argument and became the basis for the debasing theories of the Nazis concerning the Jews. It became necessary to take a group of people defined completely by social and cultural characteristics and ascribe physical differences to them in order to establish justification for their mass murder.

This tendency in western culture to strip the mantel of humanity from those we intend to kill begins with vocabulary. We cease to refer to potential victims in familiar, human terms, and we adopt new words such as "gooks" for Vietnamese communists or "fetal tissue" instead of baby. This is why, even to this day, the word "nigger" stings like a whip.

In the American colonies, the plantation system contributed to the complete moral deterioration of the white community. Because only blacks could be fully enslaved, an absolute equation grew between plantations and slavery, slavery and race. Legal fictions were used as justification backed by the previously mentioned spurious claims of ethnic superiority. But the root of the system was greed and economic necessity, brought about by the heavy debt incurred in capitalizing the estates.

The invention of the cotton gin by Eli Whitney at the end

of the eighteenth century guaranteed the expansion of cotton cultivation and the slave system in the new southern American states. Money was to be made and early doubts were trampled underfoot in the rush to prosperity.

But Now I See

The battle to end slavery began in an unlikely setting. In London, the horrors of slavery were remote and unseen; few argued against one of the nation's most bountiful sources of wealth. After all, cotton and sugar profits were very tangible. Consciences were untouched by the suffering of blacks in remote places; they had enough suffering close at hand in the dark mill towns of the Industrial Revolution. However, God had chosen a man.

One of the disciples of Wesley was a politician named William Wilberforce. He and his evangelical friends spent their adult lives in a relentless campaign against slavery. They distributed thousands of pamphlets detailing the evils of slavery to an ignorant public, circulated petitions and spoke at public meetings. They even organized a boycott of slave-grown sugar that gained a following of 300,000 people across England.

In 1792, Wilberforce was able to bring to the House of Commons 519 separate petitions for the total abolition of slavery, signed by thousands of British subjects.

In 1807, the slave trade was outlawed throughout the British Empire and 19 years later the total emancipation of existing slaves was enacted. The merchant fleets were turned to other purposes and the mighty British navy, which once protected the trade, now policed the coast of Africa with a blockade. This represents a miracle of divine intervention of the first order. It is equivalent to the American abortion industry turning to the eradication of the international abortion industry as its chief purpose, something almost beyond imagination in our day.

How did this come about? Why were the English reformers so successful while the United States sank even deeper into entanglement with slavery? The British had just as much to lose economically; slavery was one of the great foundation stones of their international trade.

As I read the speeches and tracts of the English abolitionists, I am struck by the comparative lack of self-righteousness. Like Abraham Lincoln in a later generation, they practiced identificational repentance. Wilberforce's first parliamentary speech for abolition set the tone for so much of what was to follow.

> I mean not to accuse anyone, but to take the shame upon myself, in common, in deed, with the whole Parliament of Great Britain, for having suffered this horrid trade to be carried on under their authority. We are all guilty—we ought all to plead guilty, and not to exculpate ourselves by throwing the blame on others.[2]

Wilberforce's words echo the brokenness of Nehemiah, Ezra, Jeremiah and Daniel. This is the attitude that God must see before He heals a land. Too often, healing has been interrupted by those who proclaim God's truth without God's heart. The Bible reveals that it's possible to hear truth, agree with it and act on it, yet completely contradict God's nature. Look at the response of Nebuchadnezzar upon seeing the deliverance of the Hebrew children from the fiery furnace. "Therefore, I make a decree that any people, nation or tongue that speaks anything offensive against the God of Shadrach, Meshach and Abed-nego shall be torn limb from limb and have their houses reduced to a rubbish heap" (Dan. 3:29). This has often been the misguided response of the ignorant to God's authority and God's truth, from Roman Emperors and English Crusaders to Spanish Conquistadors.

We, in our generation, must not let this spirit enter our struggle with the pagans over moral issues. It would be best to start with the most glaringly obvious failure of the Church: our continuing racial divisions. The most hopeful sign I see in American Christianity is a turning away from the cheap crusading rhetoric that denounces the pagans, in favor of humble identification with them in our mutual need of God's help. If racism is the thing more than any other that reveals the spiritual poverty of the American Church, let's take up this issue as the first order of public confession.

> IF RACISM IS THE THING MORE THAN ANY OTHER THAT REVEALS THE SPIRITUAL POVERTY OF THE AMERICAN CHURCH, LET'S TAKE UP THIS ISSUE AS THE FIRST ORDER OF PUBLIC CONFESSION.

A Higher Standard

I don't know if the American people have ever grappled with the issues of race in the way England did during the 1790s. We have had awful conflicts, but have we reached a consensus shaped by the heart of God? Cornel West, director of Princeton University's Afro-American Studies, has observed, "The foundational failure of this country is to engage in a candid and critical discussion about race."[3]

During my years of public speaking, I have often been interrupted by people calling out questions, particularly this one: "What's wrong with people worshiping God in their own cultural style? Don't we remain separated on Sunday just because we are more comfortable with our way of doing things? What's wrong with that? It's only natural."

First of all, separation is not natural. Opposites do not repel, they attract. For example, whites have a profound love of black music and blacks have a deep appreciation for the emphasis on education within the European tradition. Separation only seems natural because it is all we have known. Actually, it is an indirect result of the sin/guilt/separation dynamic.

A church-planting strategy among immigrant peoples that provides the first generation with teaching and fellowship in their own native tongue is an obvious need. However, it is profoundly unnatural for believers who speak the same language and live in the same place to remain separated for hundreds of years. Even if this were not true, it is imperative that Christians living in a nation whose biggest problem is racial conflict demonstrate a prophetic prototype of the unity and love that is the unique gift of God's kingdom. If Jesus does forgive, cleanse and reconcile us, why not show it? The American Church should be, could be, the greatest celebration of cultural diversity this side of heaven. Let's have it all. Black/white reconciliation could be the foundation of a prophetic parable that embraces immigrants and broadcasts hope to the world.

Instead, 130 years after emancipation and 25 years after the Civil Rights Movement, racism is still deeply entrenched in the fabric of the North American religious landscape. A black Oral Roberts University professor, Leonard Lovett, voices a typical lament. "Had the European-American church collectively and prophetically indicted racism in word and deed decades ago, the problem of racism would have been virtually resolved."[4] Instead, we exemplify the problem.

A black/white reconciliation movement within America is beginning. Of course, veteran black leaders such as Wellington Boone, John Perkins and Joseph Garlington have been speaking out for years, but only recently has significant white leadership begun to emerge.

Think of what we learned as we explored Native American issues and apply the same truths to the African-American experience. Instead of broken treaties and battles, think of the relentless brutality of slave labor in the midst of religious hypocrisy. Instead of the site of a massacre, think of the site of a slave auction where whole families were torn from one another and sold to the highest bidder, never to be seen again. We *can* do something, there *is* hope, but the white Church must take the initiative.

In 1989, I visited a midwest city in which racially inspired injustice seemed to be the only major blot on an otherwise wholesome past. It all seemed to be focused on one shameful incident.

A white mob, outraged over an unsolved crime, lynched an innocent black man. Several people told me this story as vividly as though it had happened yesterday. The incident seemed to have lost none of its power to create guilt and bitterness even though it happened generations ago.

I described the incident in my book *Taking Our Cities for God* without mentioning the name of the town and went on to say:

> Repentance, reconciliation and healing could take place if Christians from the black and white community joined together in identification with the sins and griefs of our forbears. If the sin is acknowledged and relationship is restored, then the authority of the Lord can be exercised over the demonic forces that have been exploiting the past.
>
> The new resident of the city might think, "That's not my problem. I just moved here last year." However, when God puts you in a city you become part of the Church there and you inherit its legacy, good or bad. The unfinished business of the Church is now your responsibility, too.[5]

As the sales of *Taking Our Cities for God* began to approach 200,000 copies worldwide, I became very glad that I had not mentioned the name of the town I had described. People began to contact me from all over America, convinced that I was referring to their city. It seems that similar incidents occurred in an embarrassingly large number of places. One of the cities where believers became convinced I was telling their story was Springfield, Missouri. I received the following report.

Coming Clean

Three-thousand Christians in joyous parade walked through central Springfield as part of the 1992 March for Jesus. As they approached the public square, a mood of sobriety settled upon them. It was time to do more than thank Jesus for salvations. It was time for confession and cleansing. This same square was the place of that city's greatest shame.

■ ■ ■

It was Easter weekend of 1906, a year cursed with earthquakes (San Francisco) and blessed with revival (Azusa Street). On Good Friday, April the 13th, a white woman claimed that she was raped by Horace Duncan and Fred Coker, both black. The young men were arrested but then released the same day because the police quickly admitted they were "probably innocent." On Saturday night, due to the mounting public outcry, the men were rearrested and placed in the county jail. That same evening a mob of several thousand men and boys descended on the jail, intimidated the jailers and hauled the prisoners to the public square where they hanged and then burned them beneath a replica of the Statue of Liberty. Not fully satisfied, the lynch crowd went back to the jail and brought back a third black man, Will Allen, whom they gave a mock trial, ending with his hanging. Six thousand men, women and children looked on. Later, pictures of the town's Gottfried Tower, the three bodies inked in, were sold as souvenirs.

Springfield's black community was permanently damaged. The potential of a prosperous middle class was cut off. In the following weeks, hundreds of blacks left Springfield forever. Farms, livestock, homes and businesses were left abandoned. Years of family effort were destroyed in 48 hours of misguided white vengeance.

■ ■ ■

The March for Jesus crowd—hundreds of families as well as clergy from 25 churches—stood in the square, heads bowed. One of the white leaders began to pray.

> We ask for forgiveness for the unjust lynching of Horace B. Duncan, Fred Coker and Will Allen. We, as Your Church, repent of the mob violence and the spirit of spectatorism that took place on the Easter weekend of 1906. We ask forgiveness for the death, destruction, and devastation which was perpetuated against the black community and which was allowed to replace the celebration of Easter's life-giving res-urrection. We ask for forgiveness from the families of these men, from the hundreds of black individuals who left Springfield because of this event and from the black community at large for the fear and intimi-dation which was established in this city this dark day.
>
> We repent of our perpetuation—by sins of com-mission and omission—of the evils of racism, bigotry and prejudice, and ask for God to help us to heal the deep divisions which exist in our city.
>
> We pray for a spirit of unity and racial openness to be established once again in this city. We pray for racial diversity to be celebrated and encouraged and

for the spirit of racial hospitality to reign at the gateways of our city.

In Christ's name we pray. Amen.[6]

A black pastor responded by speaking out his forgiveness while blacks and whites embraced across the square.

The Marches for Jesus are excellent vehicles for ceremonies of repentance and reconciliation. Over the last three years, the marches have brought more black and white Christians together than any other national effort. As one of the founders of the national organization and the chairman of the advisory board, I have had an excellent chance to see God at work in this amazing movement. A march has become an occasion for cleansing and healing many times.

In September 1991, for instance, blacks and whites in St. Louis, Missouri, marched side by side to the steps of the old county courthouse where 131 years ago Dred Scott was condemned to a lifetime of slavery. There, in the rain, confession was made over past and present sins of racism and black Christians spoke out their forgiveness.

Unfinished Business

For many years I have traveled from city to city across America asking the same simple question: What went on here during the days of slavery and segregation? Have the implications ever been addressed by the united Church in any generation (in terms of corporate repentance)? Amazingly, in spite of a bloody Civil War, years of national political debate, deepening inner-city crisis, unprecedented unity among believers and a born-again population approaching 40 percent, I have failed to find a single city that has done anything until very recently.

It's time for a little research and a lot of action. Racial harmony will never be attained through polite ceremonies and integrated events, and nothing will happen at all unless we begin a deeper process. Many believers have memories of sitting in some convention center with a racially mixed audience and African-American speakers on the program; but I ask you, were the root issues ever addressed in a biblical way, with a level of repentance likely to produce true healing?

What about the cities of the north or the west? Regional self-righteousness won't wash with God; honest research will reveal no basis for it. For instance, some of the most severe national wounds were inflicted by organized bodies of believers acting in racial superiority or hatred, and many of these things took place far from the south.

I recently addressed a national convention of the Lydia prayer movement. During the afternoon, the women paired off and went on a prayer walk through the streets of old Philadelphia near our hotel. Three women—two white, one black—found themselves standing before a Colonial-era church, St. George's Methodist Espiscopal.

When they entered, a strange sorrow overcame them and they began to weep. They felt it necessary to ask their black sister to stand in proxy for her people and the two white women asked her forgiveness for all the injustice and oppression inflicted upon African-Americans.

Unknown by the three women at the time, they were standing at the site of a historic division between black and white believers.

In 1777, a slave named Richard Allen purchased his freedom. In that same year, he was converted under the preaching of the Methodists. Allen became a disciple of Bishop Asbury and began to preach, often visiting St. George's Methodist Episcopal in Philadelphia. So many blacks began to attend the church that the local officials decided to segregate them.

One day Allen and fellow black Christian leaders occupied the "wrong" section of the gallery and while on their knees praying were pulled out of the church. This indignity led to the formation of a separate fellowship for blacks, the African Methodist Espiscopal Church, a prominent denomination to this day.

It is particularly disturbing when pastors of some of today's predominantly white denominations look at the roots of their movement and find racism as a contributing cause of its existence. Some of my friends are puzzled by the absence of God's blessing on their attempts to establish integrated congregations, and are shocked and embarrassed when I point out certain facts about their denominational foundations. There is no need for condemnation here; it's just a matter of open acknowledgment before the Lord and representatives of the appropriate part of the black community. Preferably, this should be done at a national convention, not in a back room. Let's get clean and get on with our tasks.

I recently addressed the California Convention of Southern Baptists and again heard from many present the desire to remove the word "Southern" from the denominational masthead because of its connotations. Some Southern Baptists have told me that from a historical perspective it is a statement on slavery.

Perhaps the most bittersweet memories of the American Church are those emanating from the Azusa Street Revival of 1906. Let's look at its context.

Dividing the Healing Stream

The years 1880-1914 are often considered the worst period in Afro-American history. Retaliation came after reconstruction. Frustration, bitterness and despair replaced optimism and hope when the north, preoccupied with its rapid industrial development, returned the black man to the control of his former master and to a condition little better than slavery.

At great personal cost, northern, and a few southern, white men and women set up schools to teach the free blacks, but by and large the white crusaders for racial justice and democracy became weary and made little protest when political maneuvering effectively placed southern whites back into a position of total social dominance.

This period saw a return to institutionalized forms of racism—the enactment of rigid laws requiring discrimination and segregation in all aspects of American life. The same churches that had vociferously championed the abolition of slavery turned their backs on the liberated slaves, and the evils that haunt race relations to this day found their root.

Into this dark night of apathy, hatred and despair blazed the bright light of God's intervening grace. Surely it is divine providence that the old Shoshone Indian place name, Azusa, means "blessed miracle."

The Azusa Street Revival was a modern Pentecost in which the outpoured Spirit broke the barriers to true Christian unity. Racial division, America's greatest problem, was swept away. The huge (900 capacity) dirt-floor barn that housed William Seymor's church attracted scores of ethnic groups from their separate enclaves across Los Angeles. At one communion and foot-washing service, which went on all night, 20 nationalities participated.

Brother Seymor was a black evangelist who had arrived in Los Angeles from Houston, only to be rejected by the small church that had invited him to be their pastor. He formed a home prayer-group among black friends and on three climactic days amid a 10-day fast glossolalia and other charismatic phenomena burst forth. The crowds of curious people became too big for the house and the ramshackle former livery stable on Azusa Street was rented. The whole course of history was about to change.

Only two years later the outflow of this movement had

taken root in more than 50 countries. Every city in the United States had been affected, and literature that spread the message was published in 35 languages from Iceland to Tasmania. However, there was controversy.

Glossolalia was not the issue. Seymor was visited by an old white friend—a veteran of the Pentecostal phenomenon that had broken out in a small Bible school in Topeka, Kansas—in the early hours of January 1, 1901; the dawn of the twentieth century. He saw something in Seymor's barn that deeply disturbed him. People were lying on the floor like "a forest of fallen trees" in apparent trances—and they were of a variety of races. Chinese, Native American, white, black and Latino seemed oblivious to the "violation of Scripture" in which they were participating.

This sincere and loving man—Seymor's friend—was afflicted with the blindness of his generation. He admired the Ku Klux Klan and believed that the besetting sin of humanity was racial mixing. He believed the great flood to be God's judgment on this sin and that Noah had been chosen because he was "without mixed blood." After denouncing Seymor, he continued in his ministry, preaching against racial mixing and proclaiming the baptism in the Holy Spirit to all who would hear.

Seymor was undaunted. He believed that the coming together of the races was the essential thing God was accomplishing and the fact that it was occurring between the two groups most at odds (poor whites and poor blacks) was proof of a divine visitation.

As the movement grew, opposition increased from traditional white denominations who discredited the baptism of the Spirit by arguing that it was a by-product of black emotionalism and couldn't possibly be genuine. In order to remove the stigma of these humble black beginnings, Pentecostals divided into two groups, one black and one white, between 1908 and 1914. Glossolalia became the new emphasis, and the new source of controversy, and God's true purpose went down the memory hole. The fact remains that the Pentecostal-charismatic renewal began as a gift of God through the black church to this troubled nation, a movement that now includes more than 100 million people in every nation.

Satan is terrified by the prospect that the historic stream, including Methodists, the Holiness Movement, Pentecostals and charismatics, will, through repentance, reclaim their lost heritage and begin to function according to the grace that God had originally given them. Even as it was during the original Pentecost in Jerusalem, so it could be in today's Church. At the first Pentecost, a great diversity of peoples were bound together in love, becoming the foundation of the New Testament Church.

The very hopelessness that permeates the national mood at this time only serves to accentuate the urgency with which we need to pursue reconciling efforts within the Church. In spite of our history, God will give us another chance. His mercy is fathomless. The same healing, cleansing, reconciling Holy Spirit that was poured out at Azusa Street is hovering over the nation, ready to be released—if we will just look up and see God's purpose.

Los Angeles has become a nightmare glimpse into a possible future, a metaphor for all that has gone wrong with America. But God has not abandoned the place where He once poured out His Spirit.

Six months before South Central Los Angeles erupted in flames, 10,000 of us gathered there. We represented the whole spectrum of denominations, and I counted 35 languages as people on the platform prayed for our city in their native tongues. This was the kingdom of God. Korean arms linked around African bodies, tears of love and forgiveness flowing, Mexican and Jew, Lebanese and Lithuanian, a self-confessed southern redneck, prominent among the organizers. What stark contrast to the brooding tensions building outside that auditorium.

The secular culture of Los Angeles seemed sunk into a hopeless, leaderless pessimism, but the Church had never been so united. We, like Esther, had been purified and beautified in the King's back rooms for such a time as this. As terrible as the riots were, they represented a small part of a much more devastating potential. Both before and after the riots, God's people were a bee-hive of fellowship and mutual assistance across racial lines. For all the shame and embarrassment Christians feel about this city, we also feel a rising tide of joy as we discover the new gifts of friend-ship this crisis has fostered among us.

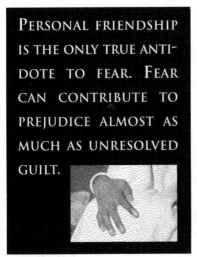

PERSONAL FRIENDSHIP IS THE ONLY TRUE ANTI-DOTE TO FEAR. FEAR CAN CONTRIBUTE TO PREJUDICE ALMOST AS MUCH AS UNRESOLVED GUILT.

The book of Acts records the way the united believers of many cultures behaved during the Jerusalem Pentecost. "So continuing daily with one accord in the temple, and breaking bread from house to house, they ate their food with gladness and simplicity of heart" (Acts 2:46, *NKJV*).

Acts 2:46 reveals the key. In the wake of the Los Angeles riots, God's people rediscovered the importance of the simple things. Nothing breaks down barriers like having people over and sharing a meal. High-minded rhetoric finds its final fulfill-ment when kids sleep over, families of different races play and vacation together, and we find ourselves participating in funer-als, graduations and weddings, the rituals of family passage.

Personal friendship is the only true antidote to fear. Fear can contribute to prejudice almost as much as unresolved guilt. The grotesque images of looting and arson, particularly the beat-ing of Reginald Denny at Florence and Normandy, sent a ripple of raw fear through white America. Hatred is fear's companion and now waits in the shadows for summons. The Bible says, "Perfect love casts out fear" (1 John 4:18), instructing us on the antithetical nature of fear and love. That which we fear we will soon come to hate; so it is in Satan's best interest to propagandize us with that which will not only cause us to fear himself, but also to fear some element of society from whom he is trying to alienate us.

Satan is a masterful liar and knows that lies work best against a backdrop of ignorance. People groups can become suffused with a jumble of inner vows with which they judge the actions of other people groups. They are sure they "know" the other group, but do they? In the absence of true communication, Satan is able to fill the silence with his own whispered interpretation of reality, manipulating our minds by amplifying the voices of strident people and elevating extreme events with a view to provoke hatred and deepen distrust.

It is common for unclean spirits to "stage" events that play to our worst fears. I remember when a young white family from northern California came to live and work with us. They came from a monocultural town. (My wife, who is from the same place, reports that there were only two black students in her entire high school.)

During their first week with us, the family went shopping at the local market. While backing his small car out of a parking space, my friend had the misfortune of nudging a large dilapidated Cadillac that was also maneuvering out of its parking space. A very drunk, very angry, very large black man dressed like a pimp from a '60s movie leaped out of the car, brandishing a baseball bat. My friend was subject to a tirade of threats as he cowered in his tiny car with his terrified wife and his wide-eyed, red-headed children.

When I heard about the incident, I burst out laughing. "That never happens," I told him. "That kind of thing only happened to me when I first moved here; it's Satan playing to your fears. Ignore it and receive the wonderful African-American friends that God is about to give you."

■ ■ ■

Notes

1. Susanne Everet, *History of Slavery* (Secaucus, New Jersey: Chantwell Books, Inc., 1992).
2. Charles Colson, *Kingdoms in Conflict* (Grand Rapids, MI: Zondervan, 1988), p. 102.
3. John Allen Chalk, "Racism," *Wineskins* magazine, August 1991, Nashville, TN.
4. Leonard Lovett, "The Black College Renaissance," *Ministries Today* magazine, July/August 1991, Lake Mary, FL.
5. John Dawson, *Taking Our Cities for God* (Lake Mary, FL: Creation House, 1989).
6. Permission to use from March for Jesus U.S.A., Austin, TX, regarding event on May 23, 1992. Report compiled by Springfield M.F.J. committee.

17

YEAH, BUT??

Answers to Common Objections

At this point, you probably have some serious questions. Most people do when I speak on the subject of reconciliation in a seminar. Here are answers to some of the most asked questions. Let's talk.

I still can't understand why you, a New Zealander, would ask a black person for forgiveness for the wounds of slavery. Your ancestors didn't come from here, you weren't born here, you're not even a citizen yet.

Of course there are those whose identity puts them in a more powerful position than me. For instance, I have met people who still possess certificates of ownership for slaves as part of their family memorabilia. But it is also true that Christians coming to live in a region become fully identified with their new family in God and inherit the unfinished business of the Church in that region.

I have found that my pride always wants to narrow the category of identification in order to find a way out, while the humility of the indwelling Christ inclines me toward widening the category in order to get in. Perhaps my citizenship distances me from the issue, but my Anglo-Saxon ethnicity binds me firmly to both the guilt of the slave owner and the grandeur of the abolitionist crusaders. A reconciler's most powerful tools are found within his or her own identity.

Does this mean I have to ask every black person I meet for forgiveness just because I'm white?
Of course not. Do what love and wisdom dictates in any given circumstance.

How do we as Afro-American Christians respond to all this; it seems that white Christians need to take the initiative.
That's true. Hopefully, the next 10 years will be a needed catharsis for the American Church as we finally face this issue honestly and receive healing. At times, your role as a black believer will be to simply receive public and private words of confession and extend forgiveness. It is important to let God move. If people are humbling themselves, let it happen; don't cut short the deep work God is doing because it feels a little awkward. You *can* stand in proxy for your whole race even though you may feel preposterous doing so. Some Afro-American Christian leaders have found themselves in this position over and over again recently.

Your emphasis on the unique attributes of peoples has been used by despots like Hitler to devastate humanity.

Aren't people really all the same? Isn't equality really the highest value?

The idea of equality should not make us afraid of discovering and affirming unique gifts within individuals or peoples. Equality should not be equated with uniformity. If you and I are identical in every way, our value is not enhanced, it is diminished. With what will we serve each other if we bring no essential difference to our relationship? This of course is most evident in marriage—we find the opposite sex both attractive and necessary because of their essential otherness.

IDENTITY MUST BE BASED ON THE IDEA OF CONTRIBUTION: THE UNIQUE GIFTS WITHIN NATIONS AND PEOPLE BEING USED TO SERVE OTHERS.

I acknowledge there is a dark side to this. When we observe traits within peoples, we encounter the danger of negative stereotyping. That which is praiseworthy in somebody else's group identity should never be seen as a limitation on the individual within that group. To return to our example of gender: just because women are observed to be nurturing by nature, it does not follow that they should be judged unfit for the harsh realities of leadership.

The other great danger of stereotyping is when a people group uses its special identity to justify immoral actions. The unique giftings within peoples should never become the basis for a self-congratulatory notion of superiority. This was the great sin of Adolf Hitler. He mobilized his nation by manipulating the search for identity. He suggested that the distinctive traits within German culture implied a right of dominance. He first concluded that these traits were superior rather than complementary to other cultures and then advocated a theory of German political dominance based on Darwin's principle of the survival of the fittest.

Identity must be based on the idea of contribution: the unique gifts within nations and peoples being used to serve others. The alternative is identity defined by grievance. This speaks to the main concern that many thinkers have expressed over the plethora of ethnic study departments springing up on today's American campuses. These departments are only valid if the end goal is to release the contribution of a people group into the wider society. It is our contribution that brings us dignity, not an inward focus on our own particulars.

> THE CHRISTIAN PERSPECTIVE ALWAYS BEGINS WITH CREATION AND ANCHORS ITS UNDERSTANDING IN THE GOD WHO HAS SPOKEN.

What about racial intermarriage? Won't that confuse identity and produce people who feel that they don't belong to anybody?

No. Children of mixed blood (technically speaking that's all of us) just find their identity in a bigger group, such as the city or the nation-state. Intermarriage strengthens America. Children with more than one heritage have not lost, they have gained. My own boys, for example, have been enriched with wider roots going deep into the soil of history. The broader the base, the more can be built on it.

Why dwell so much on the past? Why not ignore the whole mess and get on with life? Isn't that the only way to survive?

It is because of our concern for the future that we must deal with the past. Denial is dangerous. As Christians, we have a mandate from God to disciple nations. This means providing leadership, and leadership involves planning for the future by establishing worthy goals.

The process of finding direction is similar to the process of aiming a firearm. The all-important factor is the distance between the notch and the bead as two points of reference placed along the gun barrel. This is why a Derringer is inaccurate in contrast to a long-barreled rifle. Imagine that the bead is equivalent to this moment in time and we are aiming at a goal in the future, such as preserving our nation for our children. Our success will depend on the perspective gained by stepping back in time and viewing God at work in the American past. The farther back we go, the greater the wisdom gained. Indeed, the Christian perspective always begins with Creation and anchors its understanding in the God who has spoken. Ours is a culture of remembrance because we are a people of covenant.

You have mostly explored the dark side of the American story with emphasis on the repentance of Anglo-Christians. Is this an accurate version of U.S. history? Is this balanced?

I cannot write or teach from some omniscient standpoint. I cannot pretend to be God on high. A point of view is a view from a point and when dealing with the subject at hand it is particularly important that I clearly identify myself as a white male, Anglo-Saxon, Protestant Christian, and deal primarily with the issues that flow from such an identity. It is up to Christian leaders in other racial and cultural categories to lead out in repentance in order to cleanse the group they represent.

An example of this occurred in March 1993, in the meeting hall of a Southern California Indian tribe. During an intertribal gathering, Christian representatives from each of 10 tribes stood in turn before the entire group and publicly repented for tribal wounds and offenses committed against each other. Each leader went on to repent for their tribe's part in shamanism and spiritual issues that have defiled their nation, people and land. In return, the group as a whole responded verbally, in unison, accepting the apology and blessing that tribe.

It is beyond me to bring a balanced commentary on the

virtues and weaknesses of America's subcultures, but it *is* my duty to embrace the dark side of my own subculture even though I may see clearly the need for repentance in others. For instance, I am well aware of the African-American struggle with resentment, even hatred, of whites, and that the most overt racism in this generation is sometimes practiced by black people. I have experienced all these things, perhaps more than most white Americans. I know that fostering bitterness is a sin and that there is a need for African-Americans to forgive and forget, but I have heard that truth eloquently expressed by black leaders many times. My obligation, as a white man, is to provide maximum grace for forgiveness by humbling myself and asking for it. It is very hard to forgive if you never hear acknowledgment of the things that have hurt you or your people group.

It is profound paradox when those who have given their whole lives to represent correctly the character of God identify in confession with those who have defamed His name the most. But that is the biblical role of the interceding reconciler. This is why an Anglo intercessor confesses the sins of the secular or nominally Christian-Anglo culture.

I acknowledge that there is a vast difference between the behavior of the genuine followers of Jesus as opposed to those who are mere members of western Christian civilization. Indeed, it is wrong to think of the past as a golden era for Christianity. The Christian community has surged in numbers during times of awakening, but at no time has it represented anything like a majority of Americans. Truly committed believers have historically been a covenantal remnant within a nominally Christian culture, as we are today. We do not practice identificational repentance because we hold the Christians of the past to be those who are primarily responsible for the unjust actions of the nation. Indeed, committed believers represent the historic nucleus for resistance to injustice. It is in our role as reconcilers that we identify with the dark side, Anglos going first because, "For everyone to whom much is given, from him much will be required" (Luke 12:48, *NKJV*).

Part of my motive is a desire to cleanse my own people group. My main concern, however, is to see repentance and confession in the Church, in order to vindicate God's character in the eyes of the pagans. The kingdom of God will be vilified publicly as long as self-righteousness marks our relationship with the world and each other.

Recently, the *Los Angeles Times* reported on the work of the researcher, Randall Wright. In one week of monitoring prime-time TV programs, he noted that God had been censored from programming except for 158 profane references. God Himself, therefore, is the ultimate victim of irrational prejudice and the bearer of the deepest wounds of rejection. Resentment toward God is animated by the same root of unresolved guilt that aggravates white/black relationships. The media industry is full of people who wear a veil of shame because of personal, moral compromise and participation in projects that glorify violence, lust and lawlessness.

Out of unresolved guilt flows the insidious tendency to transfer blame to others and ultimately to God. Through the cross, Jesus has made possible the breaking of this cycle. He has freed us to be honest, and the practice of confession advertises that fact to a world wrapped in the chains of self-deception.

Doesn't the Bible teach that each person is responsible for his or her own actions? Why should I be punished for what my ancestors did?

I'm not arguing for punishment or retribution. It is true that the individual is not responsible for events beyond his or her control. It is clearly a mistake to equate a person's heritage with complicity—to attach blame to individuals merely because of their origin. The intercessor freely chooses to identify with and to confess sin because such action often releases healing grace in the hearts of bitter people. We also acknowledge that every heritage comes with both benefits and responsibilities, including the responsibility to right past wrongs.

■ ■ ■

18

LEFT, RIGHT!
LEFT, RIGHT!

Ideological Conflict

Wisdom calls aloud outside; She raises her voice in the open squares. She cries out in the chief concourses, at the opening of the gates in the city she speaks her words.

Proverbs 1:20,21 *(NKJV)*

Racial conflict may be the most visible division in American life, but we must move on. The principles we have learned in dealing with racism can be applied to all the categories of societal conflict listed on pages 117-118. However, one category touches all the others: the ideological conflict between left and right. The black community, more than any other, has become a political football kicked around by theorists who, armed with statistics from the inner cities, evoke the black experience as the positive proof of their views.

Liberal spokesmen, promoting more government as a solution to problems, have only aggravated racial tensions. To many

poor and middle-class whites, liberalism has come to mean taking the side of blacks, no matter what—handcuffing the police
and rationalizing rioting; welfare dependency and family disintegration as "caused" by the urban environment, or as a justifi-
able response to past oppression.

People are weary of politics. The process itself has become
synonymous with breaking open old wounds. At the end of the
twentieth century, the Christian community feels brutalized by
its brief sojourn at the center of the political stage. An enormous expenditure of energy has largely resulted in disappointment. We feel misunderstood and rejected. How could a community that has love as its foundational value end up vilified
and rejected? We represent neither left nor right; how could
we be so misunderstood?

We all hope that our political leaders will find ways of both
liberating the potential of individuals and fostering benevolent
communities. Yet, along with most Americans, we gaze uncom-
fortably upon the champions of the left and the right as they
hammer at each other with self-righteous denunciation. Partisans on the right find it inexplicable that anyone could fail to
understand their insistence on hard work and personal responsibility, and partisans on the left cannot understand how anyone
could reject their insistence on tolerance and compassion. Both
expect too much of politics as a force for change.

Worst of all is the 40-year decline in the deliberative
process—a process by which people examined the facts, solved
problems and moved forward. The New England town meeting
and its offspring have been replaced by the 30-second "sound
bites" on the evening news, in which politicians polarize the citizenry in order to advance themselves. Complex problems that
need thoughtful consideration have been replaced by "issues,"
the simplified banners of party conflict.

The strongholds of the left are the media and the courts.
The middle-class struggle to maintain a standard of living is

routinely denounced as pure selfishness, and concern over rising crime rates and failed welfare programs is dismissed as covert racism. Liberal commentators and columnists fail to see that those who are complaining about government waste are not all antigovernment reactionaries, and those crying out for restoration of "traditional values" are not all bigots trying to put a straitjacket on free expression. While left and right have raised the volume of accusation, power has leaked away

THE GREAT CHALLENGE WE FACE AS WE WALK TOWARD THE YEAR 2000 IS TO DISCIPLE THIS NATION [UNITED STATES] THE WAY GOD WOULD DO IT—IN SHORT, TO GET THE CHURCH TO ACT LIKE JESUS.

from the electoral process and more and more questions are settled by the courts.

If there has ever been a time when Americans wanted less political posturing and polarizing rhetoric, it is now. People are turning away from the politicians, searching for change, yet trusting no one.

And the Church?

This is a period similar to the end of the 1960s, just before the Jesus Movement. At that time, the mood of the Church almost aborted what God was trying to do. We were so scandalized by long hair, free love and loud music that we interpreted the counterculture as the living proof of the end of the age. "Hold the fort for the Antichrist cometh! Lock up your kids, store food in the hills, the hairy unwashed barbarians are among us!"

To our surprise, counterculture youth turned out to be the element of our society most vulnerable to the gospel. Thanks only to the pursuing mercy of God, these prodigals suddenly appeared in the front three rows of our churches. One of the most promiscuous, lawless generations in American history came into the Kingdom in spite of, not because of, the Church.

Will the prophets of paranoia radicalize the Church again? Will today's searching New Ager, wounded feminist or angry ethnic see a wall of rejection when they look around for Jesus? Satan's greatest fear is that a generation in transition will look away from their idols and see love in the eyes of the Church. As we have seen, fear and love are opposites. Satan wants to use fear to cast out love from the heart of the reconciler.

Obviously, the great challenge we face as we walk toward the year 2000 is to disciple this nation the way God would do it—in short, to get the Church to act like Jesus.

To me, one of the most amazing things about God is His self-control. He could have used raw power to shake humanity, but He has chosen to woo His creation through loving-kindness instead. The Bible reveals the way God has patiently reached out to fallen societies. From Abraham to Paul, He has taken the culture of each generation as He found it, and then chosen His friends, through whom He progressively reveals Himself.

The emancipation of women is a case in point. Honored leaders such as King David had more than one wife, and initially polygamy and other forms of male oppression seemed to go unchallenged. But God steadily built upon the foundation of His revealed purpose until a generation came along (the time of the New Testament Church) in which polygamy resulted in automatic disqualification from the ministry, and women were held in high esteem.

Slavery was treated the same way. Some forms of this institution continued, even among biblical characters who honored God, until the power of the resurrected Christ began to bring true change to master/slave relationships. This change came not by law, but voluntarily from the heart, as in the case of Onesimus and Philemon.

Polarization

We live in strange times.

An unmarried couple in their 20s is spending the day on Puget Sound in Washington state. The sailboat glides across the green depths in the summer heat like a dreamer's fantasy. She is downstairs slipping into her bathing suit while he consults the cloudless sky. There are no edges to his thoughts right now, only the pleasant numbness of the wine and a feeling of satiation. They have just made love, a few minutes ago, back at the anchorage. The word "fornication" never entered their minds. They simply expressed affection for one another in the giving and taking of sexual pleasure.

Smiling at her man, she emerges with the ice tray and two glasses, placing them beside him on the seat cushion. "Pass me a soda," she purrs. He flips open the icebox and snags the remainder of the six-pack with one finger, pulling free the two remaining cans. He then leisurely spins the plastic collar overboard like a frisbee. The six plastic rings touch down in the glistening wake and her eyes darken with anger.

"How could you do that!" she shrieks, and a bitter argument shatters the summer tranquility. He has violated the sacred gospel of environmental preservation—in broad daylight, in front of a witness. Surely this is sin.

I have often heard Christians mock today's values by using such anecdotes. They lament the blindness of the popular culture, particularly the "looney" left, but we need to be careful here. Remember Satan's strategy? (See page 107.)

Take some truth; polarize the people with different sides of that truth;...watch them wound each other with rejection and harsh words.

We must identify with people engaged in any praiseworthy pursuit at the point where their actions are biblical. To go back to the previous example, we are not in disagreement with efforts to preserve the ecosystem. On the second page of our Bibles we see God placing Adam and Eve in the garden "to cultivate it and keep it" (Gen. 2:15). Environmental stewardship is an ancient biblical mandate, not a new concept arising from the community of enlightened science in the twentieth century. Scientific discovery about the interdependency of living things only confirms the virtues of self-control and careful management espoused in the Bible.

I want you to look again at a passage of Scripture you may have read many times. Romans 12:17-21 reads:

> Never pay back evil with evil to anyone. Respect what is right in the sight of all men. If possible, so far as it depends on you, be at peace with all men. Never take your own revenge, beloved, but leave room for the wrath of God, for it is written, "Vengeance is Mine, I will repay," says the Lord. "But if your enemy is hungry, feed him, and if he is thirsty, give him a drink; for in so doing you will heap burning coals upon his head."* Do not be overcome by evil, but overcome evil with good.

---

*This did not imply retribution. Live coals were often carried home on the heads of the ancients, contained in an earthen pot. This passage refers to the kindness of one who helps to keep the fire burning.

Indeed, this is a rich passage, full of things applicable to our discussion, but look at the small phrase in verse 17: "Respect what is right in the sight of all men."

Beneath the surface of bitter factional debate there is usually at least some degree of truth on both sides. It is these elements of truth that Satan uses as the hook for deceptive and polarizing ideologies. For instance, communism advertised itself as the source of justice and security for the laboring masses. The goal itself was noble, and communism drew millions of well-meaning people into its orbit before the hope it had generated was revealed to be a false hope.

Sometimes truth is found in the strangest places. Prominent in today's headlines is a religious leader who preaches black self-reliance, rejects welfare dependency and often states that the underlying problem in the black community is the hopelessness and inferiority that stems from rejection.

No, that's not Martin Luther King Jr., or E. V. Hill or even Malcolm X. The voice is that of Nation of Islam's Louis Farrakhan, a leader who is often castigated in the press for his more radical views. In his own way, he is speaking to the root problem confronting black Americans. "A wounded spirit who can bear?" (Prov. 18:14, *KJV*).

We must honor truth where we find it. We must affirm those who speak it even if they usually oppose us. I'm sure it offends God when we vilify the entire motivation and reject the entire thought and contribution of persons and movements that do not adhere to all of our agenda. It is tempting to completely reject persons who hold destructive ideas and do things that we don't agree with, but Jesus doesn't reject us. We may feel that we have more truth than an Islamic zealot or an American Civil Liberty Union activist, but how do we look to God? All of us fall short of *His* understanding. Error is just a matter of degree.

Jesus reserved His intolerance for unrepentant religious insiders (the Pharisees), and dealt with outsiders with tact, patience and compassion. Even more remarkably, when Jesus taught on compassion He chose a Samaritan for commendation, a truly radical violation of Jewish sensibilities. To the Jews, the Samaritans were despised heretics.

Mankind is fallen and in need of God, but relatively few people are self-consciously evil. Most people see themselves as having at least some virtues. In addition to that, most people honor certain virtues they themselves do not possess. It is when people see themselves as supporting something noble that they are capable of the most unyielding tenacity and seemingly unresolvable conflicts are born. A case in point is the clash over abortion. I have come to call this conflict mercy and justice versus mercy and justice.

WHEN EVERY TRIBE, KINDRED AND TONGUE IS UNITED AROUND THE THRONE OF GOD, WE WILL SEE THE ANSWER TO ALL THE YEARNINGS OF THE HUMAN HEART DOWN THROUGH THE AGES.

The proponents of abortion rights certainly do not see themselves as evil. They see themselves as compassionate humanitarians concerned for the poor quality of life experienced by unwanted children and rejected women. Yet, when a Christian protestor waves a placard that accuses proponents of abortion rights of sanctioning murder, that Christian is stating a moral truth. The challenge we face is to communicate truth without judging the individual; to uphold standards without taking up the satanic pattern of condemnation and accusation.

Proabortion people are living out their own moral code. It is a code derived from a mechanistic, deterministic, atheistic worldview, but it is perceived as loving and just nonetheless. It is therefore imperative that you and I see and commend the praiseworthy qualities within our ideological opponents, to denounce falsehoods and at the same time honor people who seek justice and love, to "respect what is right in the sight of all men" (Rom. 12:17).

I see Satan manipulating four issues to his advantage. His ultimate goal is intergenerational conflict in Christian homes: to alienate us from our own children. Every child who watches television or attends a public school is receiving an indoctrination, not against values, but into new values. A conflict is being set up:

1. Family values versus protection for abused individuals;
2. Environmentalism versus liberty and personal stewardship;
3. America's foundational heritage versus multiculturalism;
4. Patriotism versus globalism.

In all four of these conflicts, Christians should find themselves in what might be called the "radical middle." Take for instance patriotism versus globalism.

The long-running television series *Star Trek* is a humanistic fantasy. The peoples of the earth are united at last. Enlightened and tolerant, they have transcended the violent depravity of the human past as they participate in the conquest of space. These fictional characters, and myriad secular media, echo a yearning for one world in which reconciled peoples are served by a wise and just government.

A destructive paranoia often grips Christians at the very mention of the phrase "one world" because of its association with the coming Antichrist. But the far greater truth is that of the transcendent kingdom of God described in the book of Revelation. When every tribe, kindred and tongue is united around the throne of God, we will see the answer to all the yearnings of the human heart down through the ages. There *will* be one world, there *will* be a uniting of the nations. It's not the dream that is evil; it is the false means of achieving it.

Only Christians possess the ability to be loyal citizens of the United States and to strive valiantly for the establishment of a transcendent global Kingdom. Christians are already the most successful globalists in history. The followers of Christ are found in more cultures, language groups, nations and geographic locales than any other group. We are deeply committed to our home nations but compelled by Christ's missionary command to become servants to all the nations.

Little Boxes

For too long, we have played into the enemy's hands by allowing the secular pundits to put all believers in boxes with labels such as "the religious right" or "fundamentalists." We have allowed them to propagate a distorted report of what we believe. They use derogatory terms such as "puritanical," and other buzz words that have migrated from their original meaning and now stand for a cold, self-righteous religion in much of the public mind. Christianity is constantly accused of fostering intolerance but it is only intolerant of attempts to redefine its own essence. Absolute truth about God *can* be communicated by very tolerant people. Jesus is the supreme example of this.

There are giants of opposition in the land whose persecution comes in the form of subtle lies. As David took Goliath's own sword and beheaded him with it, so we—if we are wise—may use the very weapons that have been used to attack the Church to rout our spiritual enemy. If the enemy's sword is accusation toward us because Christians are seen to have failed to be relevant, just, and loving in some area, let us remove his power by open confession and then exploit the moral issues that have been raised as a platform for righteous action and the proclamation of biblical truth.

We need to demonstrate a "corporate" humility while upholding truth. Public moralizing without identificational repentance will only be seen as self-righteous arrogance.

I'm not talking about withdrawing from confrontation such as the hard-nosed efforts to protect religious liberties as defined by the Constitution. I applaud the work of Jay Sekulow, an attorney, and others like him who fight tooth and nail against the creeping secularism that would seek to ban all religious expression from the public arena. Nor can we be silent about the divisive moral issues of our day. But the voice of the Church should sound like the voice of the biblical Jesus.

If we become involved in politics (and surely we must), we must avoid falling into well-established categories. We must distance ourselves from automatic association with the grizzled warriors, camped out around the banners of the left and the right, and choose an obedience to Christ instead. A study of the life of Jesus reveals a person who was violent in the heavenlies, a subtle user of parables when conducting intellectual debate and a Man who stewarded His physical strength in gentleness and restraint.

> "Look at my Servant. See my Chosen One. He is my Beloved, in whom my soul delights. I will put my Spirit upon him, and he will judge the nations. He does not fight nor shout; he does not raise his voice! He does not crush the weak, or quench the smallest hope; He will end all conflict with his final victory, and his name shall be the hope of all the world" (Matt. 12:18-21, *TLB*).

The terms "leftist" and "rightist" have become almost
meaningless, often used only as firebrands of accusation hurled
by posturing politicians. Because these terms mean many different things to many different people, those who honor God's
Word will sometimes find themselves in the company of those
labeled "leftist" and sometimes in the company of those on the
right. Take, for example, the issues of racism or public education. On such issues we need to hold uncompromisingly to biblical values, even if a whole culture mocks us. However, it is
imperative that we provide maximum opportunity for our opponents to understand our position and find agreement with our
goals. This is achieved by communicating with love, wisdom
and humility in the way Jesus did.

Ideological conflict is dehumanizing; it turns real human
beings into mere "opponents." Yet, our opponents are all people
whom Jesus loves. For example, there are people who have
opposed me in Los Angeles, people who seem to harass Christians at every turn. I know God is watching me at the times I am
hurt and tempted to resentment. Will I harden my heart? If I
meet my opponent face-to-face, will she or he see love in my
eyes?

To those reading this book who are part of the liberal media
elite, I admit that I have struggled with feelings of hurt and anger
when I see believers routinely characterized as uneducated dupes
led by money-grubbing, fornicating televangelists. Look again.
Our churches are not citadels of bigotry dominated by manipu-
lative Ayatollahs. They are the legacy of those who have championed the weak and helpless for centuries, ended the slave trade,
built orphanages and hospitals and still bring to this nation something that cannot easily be replaced: an ethical consensus that
inspires us to rise beyond narrow self-interest.

Unfortunately, we Christian leaders have been equally
guilty. We have often described the liberal media from our pul-
pits as a sinister conspiracy of extremists bent on molesting our

children's minds and robbing us of religious liberty. I apologize for this. Please forgive us. This is not the framework for constructive debate. It can only hurt America and deepen the divide.

■ ■ ■

19

SEX WARS
AND OTHER
CONFLICTS

Seek peace, and pursue it.

Psalm 34:14

I noticed them crying even at a distance. There were about 9,000 of them. Nine thousand women and me.

The event took place at the Orlando Convention Center. When I finished speaking, the bolder ones approached me as I left the stage.

"Something broke in me when you said that," said one.

"You'll never know how much I needed to hear that," said another.

And then I heard the words that are all too familiar to me now: "Today is the first time I ever heard a man, any man, say, 'I'm sorry.'"

The first time I heard those words was years ago in Dallas. A woman's organization called Aglow International asked me to address their regional convention. I was intimidated at first; the only other male was a guy operating the tape machine. But they were loving people and my insecurity soon abated.

These women were remarkably open with one another as they shared stories of God's grace. As they shared, I began to empathize with them and to see with new eyes the experience of women in our time. Mostly, I just marveled at the qualities of the opposite sex. I love women, from little girls to little old ladies. They have always filled me with a sense of wonder and delight.

I was sharing these feelings in one of my teaching sessions when I realized something deeper needed to be addressed. It occurred to me that I could humble myself and ask forgiveness, as a male, for the multitude of hurts afflicted on these women by men. I was surrounded by stories of incest, rejection, betrayal and a multitude of other misogynistic actions. Why not identify with these things, bring them out into the open, confess that I knew only too well the dark side of the masculine soul?

In simple, halting words, I asked for forgiveness and I was amazed at the result. Floodgates of emotion were opened and the tears began to flow.

Dear female reader. I may not be the guy that hurt you but I look upon your hurt with shame and embarrassment, nonetheless. There have been times when I have had to ask forgiveness of mother, wife, sister and female associate. One woman in particular I would beg for forgiveness if I knew how to contact her. I am no stranger to masculine pride and male appetites. Maybe I haven't committed rape or some other loathsome offense, but it is really just a matter of degree.

Some of you were molested by your father, the ultimate parental betrayal. Some of you experienced other forms of incest and you haven't felt whole since. Most of you know what it's like to be the plaything of a teenage boy, emotionally if not physically, and nearly all of you carry some wound of rejection from a broken teen relationship or a troubled marriage.

You know what it's like to be ogled like a side of beef by someone of greater strength; to be condescended to and joked about in the presence of men. You also know what it is like to be treated tenderly but never taken seriously, your gifts spurned and your advice unheeded.

Please forgive me, forgive us. You were never meant to experience these things. They represent a gross distortion of the part of the character of God that was to be revealed to you through father, brother, husband and male friend. These things broke God's heart along with yours.

You were supposed to be adored by a loving father who praised your accomplishments and cherished the beauty of your uniqueness. You were supposed to feel unconditionally loved and completely safe in the company of male friends and relatives.

When I have confessed these things in a public gathering, I have seen such longing in the eyes of Christian men. I look around, collecting permission to speak from the eyes of my brothers. Sometimes they even shout, "Yes! Say it! That's right!"

We are so sorry; please forgive us.

It's Time for This

The crowd was bulging out into the concourse, every eye fixed on the big screen. It was one of those sports bars near the gate at the Atlanta airport. Clarence Thomas and Anita Hill were giving testimony surrounding her charges of sexual harassment against the newest candidate for Supreme Court Justice.

I pushed my way toward an empty seat and found myself sitting on the border. The room was physically and philosophically polarized. In front of me, the tables were occupied by females, behind me at the bar stood a wall of angry men. I could hear clearly the conversations in front and behind. The women were convinced that Anita Hill was telling the truth. It matched their own experience. The men were equally convinced that a good guy was getting a bad rap. "Don't get too close to a woman at work, they'll betray you every time." That day, all across America, people were renewing their inner vows.

> THE WOUNDS INFLICTED BY MEN AND WOMEN ON EACH OTHER CONSTITUTE THE FUNDAMENTAL FAULT LINE RUNNING BENEATH ALL OTHER HUMAN CONFLICT.

The wounds inflicted by men and women on each other constitute the fundamental fault line running beneath all other human conflict. If gender difference is used as the justification for the devaluation of one part of humanity, then the door is opened for the selective devaluation of all of humanity based on some difference from a perceived ideal. Gender conflict is not the main focus of this book, but I acknowledge that it is the biggest reconciliation issue of all, outside of our need to be reconciled to God the Father.

Every satanic device has been committed to the task of dividing the sexes because the male/female relationship, particularly that of husband and wife, is the essential metaphor through which God is seeking to instruct us about relationship with Himself.

"For your husband is your Maker" (Isa. 54:5). It is, therefore, imperative that we run toward this part of the battle equipped with every weapon God has given us, including identificational repentance.

One of the arguments I hear expressed is that confessing things can't be very powerful because it's just too simple. Yet, every married person knows the healing power of a few honest words. Just the other day my wife, Julie, and I were carrying the tension of an argument as we walked toward a lunch counter in the company of other missionaries. I pulled her aside and said, "Julie, I'm sorry. I overreacted. I understand what you're trying to say and why you feel the way you do."

"I'm sorry too," Julie said, and we both asked for forgiveness.

It wasn't complicated, but it was powerful. The sun burst through in our relationship. We all know that it is possible to let tensions fester unresolved for days, even months, unless we take the initiative to humble ourselves.

I am constantly amazed at the healing that is released in women when I humble myself, even if they are only hearing the words of a generic male in a public forum. I often get letters such as this one from a rejected woman and her recently molested daughter.

> Thank you for your words of confession to me. I received them with tears of gratitude and thanksgiving for God's healing. You are the first man to say them to me and I am quite sure the first man to apologize to my young daughter. She sank low in her chair when you spoke of this—I pray that God will do His healing work in her and heal countless other women tonight and elsewhere when you speak to them. Your childlike quality and sense of humor are endearing. Again, thank you for your time and your efforts. Bless you and your family. See you.
>
> Martha.

Also contributing to the grief of humanity are the wounds of same-sex rejection. Here again, you and I can help lift the wounded spirit.

While visiting friends, I was struck by the depressed mood of their teenage son. His father told me that he was a sensitive, artistic child who had never been comfortable with the macho behavior of other boys. He had never been able to understand their obsession with sports and other competitive activities and he had paid a price for not joining in. He had come to hate the school yard because of its association with harsh words. His memory was filled with taunts about his masculinity. He was beginning to wonder if he was gay.

My heart went out to him. I happened to be wearing my old rugby football shirt and was reminded of the fact that I had once been the kind of teenager that rejected him. I was the type that surfed the biggest waves, dove from high off the cliff and dared others to follow me in any physical adventure.

I called him aside and simply identified myself with that kind of exaggerated masculine behavior. I told him I was sorry and asked for his forgiveness. I told him I had come to value guys like him and that he should pursue his dreams in relation to the arts. Most of all I wanted him to see admiration in my eyes. I wanted to counter the lies of the school yard bullies, to say, "You are not rejected, you have value, we all need you, you are 'fearfully and wonderfully made' (Ps. 139:14)." These simple words seemed to touch something deep within him and I could see a wellspring of hope replacing the weight of depression.

The Reconcilers

Vocation to Vocation

Christians do amazing things when they comprehend the heart of God. Bob Willhite, a Baptist pastor, heard the voice of God speaking to his inner man. "I want you to identify with the clergy as a vocation by wearing a circular collar." This was hard to digest, for two reasons. First, it is not the custom of Baptists to be so attired and, second, the media was filled with news of two recent scandals involving preachers and he didn't really want to identify with them in public. However, he obeyed. It seemed that identification was what God was looking for.

A few weeks later he found himself asked to preach in a church near Boston Commons. As he looked out over an audience containing many street people, the story of the good Samaritan came to mind. Instead of preaching he walked off the platform and knelt in the center of the room, asking forgiveness for all the busy, preoccupied religious professionals who had passed them by.

Ragged people gathered around him, tears rolling down weathered faces. A particularly needy street person placed his arm around Bob's shoulders, pressed his face to Bob's cheek, and began speaking out his forgiveness. Many turned to Jesus that day.

It is right that preachers lead out in vocation-to-vocation reconciliation.

On one occasion, the United Pastors of Ventura County, California, had assembled at the county government center for the annual Day of Prayer. The mayors of four cities were present as well as county supervisors and other dignitaries. It was a sun-splashed day there in the manicured courtyard and the service proceeded with the quiet dignity that is fitting on such occasions. But my spirit was troubled. I was a guest, the last to speak, and the Holy Spirit was messing with my carefully prepared remarks. "You know, none of us entered the ministry because we wanted to hurt anybody," I said. "But there is not a person here today that hasn't been hurt or disappointed by somebody like me."

That day the service ended unusually. With every pastor nodding approval, I articulated our honest regrets, and asked the county's forgiveness through the people's elected representatives. A strange sense of the Lord's presence entered the courtyard when these words were spoken.

Tribe to Tribe

Undoubtedly, the most powerful demonstration of God's true nature will be shown when the world sees denominations and ministries openly reconciled. I've seen weeping evangelical and charismatic pastors ask forgiveness of each other on many occasions. And once, in Canbarra, Australia, I felt compelled to confess the arrogance, self-righteousness and anti-Catholic feeling that has often marked the movements that descended from the Protestant Reformation. I was approached by three Roman Catholic lay ministers who not only expressed forgiveness, but also poured out their hearts in confession of the sins of the Catholic community against the renewal movements of the past 500 years.

> THE BASIS FOR GENUINE UNITY AMONG DENOMINATIONS IS A UNITY OF HEART BASED ON DEEP RESPECT RATHER THAN CONDESCENDING TOLERANCE.

The Spirit of God has begun to mortar up cracks in the very foundations of our Christian heritage. In one southern city, a prominent Presbyterian minister, descendant of an unbroken line of Presbyterian ministers going all the way back to Scotland, found himself wide awake at 2:30 in the morning, penning a confession to the Methodist movement that he would later read before a citywide gathering of believers.* I quote in part:

> I speak for my people, those who went before me, and ask for forgiveness for the wrong we have done. I confess to pride that stems from our emphasis on an edu-

---

*This was done with the full approval of the executive clerk of the area presbytery and in consultation with other Presbyterian ministers.

cated clergy. We Presbyterian ministers at times felt superior to those ministers of other denominations who did not have the training we had. I confess to dependence upon the human mind and thought, at times to the neglect of listening to the Holy Spirit. I confess that we emphasize the sovereignty of God to such an extent that we tended to neglect the free-will of men and as a result we often failed to offer an altar call or to do evangelism and even on occasion ridiculed those involved in those activities. In our spiritual blindness we felt we had the truth and were not open to the truths God was revealing throughout other kinds of churches. I ask your forgiveness. I pray that we may all respect each other and rejoice in the revelation of God that each has received, thus enjoying a fullness of understanding that only diversity brings. I pray that we may honor the strengths of our own denominations while honoring the work of others. I pray that we may come together as one body, each of us enriched by the insights of the others. I pray that churches may share ministries rather than compete. I pray that we may love each other as Christ has loved us.

There is deep biblical insight in this brother's letter. He obviously sees each denomination as a bearer of redemptive gifts. He perceives a divinely ordained division of labor, equivalent to that of the Old Testament tribes. This is a positive view of church history that acknowledges the sovereignty of God in bringing to birth movements and ministries.

While acknowledging the pride and idolatry of the sectarian spirit, he, nonetheless, affirms that God has assigned redemptive purpose to each movement. This is the basis for genuine unity among denominations, a unity of heart based on deep respect rather than condescending tolerance.

There's Blood on Our Hands

There is one category we must deal with that directly involves the Church.

People who have truly followed Jesus have always been genuine lovers of the Jewish people. But it is also true that the Christian Church—in name, though not in spirit—has been responsible for much of the terrible suffering of the Jewish people.

For nearly 2,000 years parts of the Christian world relentlessly dehumanized the Jew. This helped pave the way for the Holocaust. Nazism was anti-Christian, but it gained part of its sustenance from the anti-Semitism that existed in Christendom.

In her book *Israel, My Chosen People: A German Confession Before God and the Jews,* Basilea Schlink addresses her fellow German Christians:

> How are the Jews to believe in Jesus? Have we not ourselves blindfolded them? They cannot see Jesus because of our conduct. They cannot believe in Him, because in our lives we have not presented to them the image of Jesus; rather we have shown them the image of mercilessness.

This all seems remote to the American Christian, not only because of distance in time and miles, but also because America has become the chosen home of so many Jews. Jews are among the most honored, loved members of this society.

Could it be that this distance is a grace from God that He hopes will bring a little perspective? Could it be that God expects the American Church to move beyond the ancient pattern of defensiveness and denial? Is this the time and the place for a praying remnant to take intercessory responsibility for a carnal majority in the historic Church?

It is not enough to lobby our government with requests

for Israel's fair treatment. It is not enough to show cordiality and affection to our Jewish allies in the struggle for public morals. The great historic wound to Jewish relationship is being ignored and there will never be global revival and harvest until this wound is cleansed and healed. Other aspects of Church history remain unaddressed — particularly the anti-Muslim crusades. However, the unresolved guilt of the Church in its dealings with the Jews must be one of the greatest of all hindrances to world evangelization.

Region to Region

Sometimes we miss things because they seem too grand in scale or too far back in time. I've seen intercessors weeping over things I would never have considered as we have been educated by God, while animated by the moving of His Spirit. It is hard for a person to feel deeply over a region-to-region issue, yet I've seen northerners weep with regret over the wanton destruction practiced by the Union Army during the latter part of the Civil War. I've even seen English people ask forgiveness for colonial oppression and Americans receive them with tears and hugs.

On one occasion, I saw the pastors of Riverside, California, ask forgiveness of the pastors of San Bernardino, California, for the condescending attitudes that are commonly expressed from one town to another, stemming from the earliest days of settlement.

"How far back do we go?" is the obvious question, to which I can only reply, "Do whatever God tells you to do."

Generation to Generation

Some of the wounds that most need cleansing are those inflicted by still-living generations. I remember the time when youth pastors came to Denver from all over America to consider the need for revival and harvest among teens and children. One afternoon we gathered for a prayer meeting, but the Spirit of God did not show up.

Our prayer time was so pathetic that the leaders met on the platform to ponder the evident lack of God's power. As we waited quietly for God's direction, it occurred to me that the vast majority of the conference attendees were post-World War II baby boomers, one of the most wicked generations in United States history. In the 1960s and early 1970s, we had consumed vast amounts of drugs, espoused lawlessness, rebelled against all moral restraint, indulged in rampant promiscuity and dabbled in a smorgasbord of occultic and mystical practices.

What if we were to reap what we had sown? We deserved to see our children destroyed in front of our faces. We had torn down American's walls with our own hands. Several hundred contrite youth pastors went on to acknowledge this before the Lord and immediately the prayer meeting took off with a roar. We needed to see clearly the truth about ourselves before the Spirit of truth would rest among us.

In Fort Wayne, Indiana, I was preparing to speak when weeping spread through the large crowd. As the people began to express themselves, I again heard the theme of generation-to-generation repentance. A woman in the balcony was crying out to God for mercy on our children and asking God for forgiveness for the sins of her generation. In her rebellious youth, she had been a cast member of the original production of the rock musical *Hair*—a taboo-breaking spectacle that helped promote the unrestrained lifestyles of the day.

Every generation receives the blessings and curses created for them by those who have gone before. Do our children know we have regrets? Will today's children, struggling to cope with the world we have created for them, ever hear us do more than whine about our own victimization? Only through taking responsibility for our own generation's actions can we teach them to take responsibility for theirs.

■ ■ ■

20

THE WOUNDS OF THE WORLD, AN AMERICAN INHERITANCE

The Privilege
Outweighs the Price

*"Give, and it will be given to you; good measure,
pressed down, shaken together, running over."*

Luke 6:38

It was one of those perfect Santa Barbara, California, days,
Mediterranean ambiance overlooking the blue Pacific. Inside
the hillside condo I was being served lunch. My hosts were old
friends of ours, she a Korean-American, he a European-American. Culturally, they were typical coastal Californians.

"When did your family come to America?" I said.
"When I was just a little girl," she replied, standing at the
sink, gazing out the kitchen window at things in the past.
"How do you feel about the Japanese?" I said. A look of
pain and embarrassment flickered across her face.

"Funny you should say that," she replied. "Just yesterday I was standing here at the sink remembering what happened to my relatives."

"How did you feel?" I persisted.

There was a long silence.

"Angry," she said. "I even saw hatred in my heart."

There it is. The reality of today's America. Anger and pain smoldering beneath the surface, even in a committed Christian home far from the inner cities.

America has inherited the wounds of the world. Our large cities are the greatest collections of cultural diversity ever seen. In them, Turk and Armenian, Arab and Jew, Russian and Pole, Serb and Croat, live side by side in sometimes uneasy proximity. Could the healing of these wounds be America's assignment?

Our churches are already miracles of integration in a way that we sometimes fail to comprehend.

For years, I desired to conduct a particular experiment. An opportunity finally presented itself when I found myself addressing a relatively small group of pastors in a suburban church. I started at the front row and had each person state only two of the ethnic groups within their personal heritage. By the time we got to the back of the room, we had discovered that we were in the presence of 12 Native American tribes and more than 30 peoples. You might think this group looked really "ethnic," but that was not the case. They just looked like Foursquare pastors—if you know that look.

My point is: This is no time to get discouraged. America is very young and we are already experiencing a miracle. The ethnic groups represented in that room had spent centuries tearing each other to shreds, and now they sat in unity, almost unaware of past conflicts. This is not "business as usual" for the human heart, but it is taken for granted in America—particularly in the American Church. Since 1971 I have traveled constantly through the national Church, and I can report to you that apart from the separation between black and white, this nation's churches have already arrived in a future that most of the world only dreams of.

Far more exciting than passive integration into a common culture through factors, such as intermarriage, is the recent emergence of reconcilers among the Christians of nearly every ethnic community. Let me give you an example. I received this letter in 1991.

My Personal Background

I was born in Osaka, Japan. My family immigrated to the United States in 1956. I have lived in the Los Angeles area ever since.

My Experience

I was asked to minister at a Chinese church in Westminster last November. This congregation was primarily composed of first and second generation Chinese, so that the majority spoke in Chinese and I had to speak with the aid of a translator.

Before the meeting, the Lord impressed upon my heart the need to ask forgiveness on behalf of the Japanese for the atrocities committed against the Chinese people before and during World War II. After this word came from the Lord I sensed that this might be very significant, as my father served in Manchuria with the Japanese during World War II.

Thus, I asked the people at the beginning of my ministry to forgive me on behalf of the Japanese for the acts they committed. As I spoke, the Lord seemed to give me the words to speak: "You must have been hurt deeply, losing friends and family, losing property, seeing destruction and terror." As I continued, the majority of the congregation began to weep; then, I found myself welling up with deep emotions and I, too, began to weep.

I don't quite understand the dynamics of what transpired that evening, but the Lord, indeed, gave us great release.

Here then, John, is my short testimony. Feel free to do with it as the Lord intends. In our Lord's name,
R. Shin Asami

I have used this letter in teaching and it has spawned a raft of similar letters from people who want their statements to be publicly read also, including this statement of apology and repentance from an Anglo to Japanese-Americans:

I apologize for my country and I admit the wrong to the people of Japanese ancestry during World War II. We allowed fear to dominate our decision and I ask forgiveness as an American for what our country did to you. I make no excuses for there are none.

I repent of the heartless and cruel decision that caused tragic repercussions in the lives of the Japanese/American people. We uprooted you from your homes to put you in concentration camps and treated you as enemies. You lost everything and were humiliated.

Our weak and inadequate recompense of money for all that happened to you is not enough. We unjustly accused you, convicted you, and sentenced you, collectively, as enemies of our nation.

In the Pledge of Allegiance, it states, "One nation, under God, with liberty and justice for all." We didn't adhere to our pledge. We ignored it when fear took over. We were wrong and the truth is we can't correct

the wrong to you, nor recompense you for the suffering, but I do ask your forgiveness in Jesus' name.

I embrace you as fellow Americans and sisters
and brothers in Christ. May the Holy Spirit release
and accomplish healing through repentance and forgiveness.

Madeline

America's Redemptive Purpose

Yes, there is a dream in the heart of Jesus for this nation. This
is the only nation consisting of people from every nation.
Herein lies the clue to our
destiny. I believe that
Jesus intends to demon-
strate a prototype of the
cultures of the world, reconciled to one another
and released in their gifting, and He has chosen
the American Church to
become His example in a
world without hope.

AMERICA EXEMPLIFIES BOTH
THE DANGERS AND POTENTIALS
OF THE WORLD THAT HAS COME
TO BE. THE WORLD WATCHES
OUR STRUGGLE WITH MODER-
NITY. TO THEM, WE ARE THE
FUTURE OBSERVED.

The Bible has long
foretold the dilemma of
this generation: "And in that you saw the iron mixed with common clay, they will combine with one another in the seed of
men; but they will not adhere to one another, even as iron does
not combine with pottery" (Dan. 2:43).

This passage speaks of Rome and its descendant civilization, the commercial culture of the west that dominates the
world in the end times. Here we see predicted, attempts at unity,
such as the United Nations, and the fact of increasing racial

intermarriage. Yet, outside God's kingdom there is continuous turbulence and deepening despair. America exemplifies both the dangers and potentials of the world that has come to be. The world watches our struggle with modernity. To them, we are the future observed.

I believe that God would use this nation as a springboard for global outreach, a refuge for those seeking new beginnings, and an example of the values He longs to see all peoples embrace. To the degree that we fulfill, or do not fulfill, this destiny, we will be blessed or cursed.

> THE FOREFATHERS OF AMERICA BLESSED THE WORLD WITH THEIR EXAMPLE OF JUST GOVERNMENT, BUT LEFT TO US A FLY IN THE OINTMENT THAT MADE THE WHOLE JAR STINK. BUT THIS IS THE SEASON WHEN RECONCILIATION BETWEEN PEOPLES WILL BE AMERICA'S GARLAND RATHER THAN AMERICA'S SHAME.

A Nation of Example

We are already discipling the nations. The American culture has been enriched by so many streams that it now stands astride the earth as a lone colossus. Its high-wattage allure has captured the minds of millions beyond these shores. The fight for decency in our domestic media is a fight for the world's media. Our fight for ethical answers in economics, government and law is a quest for global solutions.

In the past, America has led the way in both darkness and light, greed and generosity, decadence and purity; a staggering giant — a schizophrenic in rags with a prophet's pure dreams and a glutton's base appetites.

This land of revivals could become again the crucible of divine restoration, or it could become Babylon the Great, fallen and judged, an example of terror in the midst of the nations (see Revelation 17 and 18).

Our forefathers blessed the world with their example of just government, but left to us a fly in the ointment that made the whole jar stink. This is the season for changing that. This is the season when reconciliation between peoples will be America's garland rather than America's shame.

A Nation of Refuge

Each generation of Americans makes its choice. Will we close the doors? Will we invite the skilled and the rich but exclude the shattered and disenfranchised? Will we forget that all those except Native Americans are descendants of "boat people"? God stands ready to pour out prosperity on this nation as long as its heart is as big as His own.

We need secure borders, we need our immigration laws respected, but above all else our law and practice must remain sympathetic to the genuine refugee.

A Nation of Outreach

America continues to stand at the center of global missionary enterprise. It's no wonder when we consider that most American families carry memories of distant places and ancestral languages.

Americans so often provide the strategic leadership when international believers work together. The American gift for bold planning and excellent management has given us the feeding programs of World Vision, the medical outreach of Youth With a Mission's mercy ships, the far-ranging cultural expertise of Wycliffe Bible Translators and the evangelistic techniques of Campus Crusade for Christ. And then there are the evangelists.

The ministry of Billy Graham involves numbers that the human brain struggles to comprehend. He has already preached, in person, to more than 100,000,000 people, more than any person who ever lived. As of this writing, 2,874,082 people had responded to his call to accept Christ as their personal Savior.

Outreach has not been limited to Christian organizations. One of the greatest outpourings of American generosity was the implementation of the Marshall Plan by the United States government following World War II. Officially known as the European Recovery Plan, this amazing act of charity has been viewed by some as primarily an American attempt to stave off communism in Europe. But it was sold to the American people, state by state, at a time when communism was not seen by many Americans as a global threat. In his speeches, George Marshall stressed generosity to a devastated Europe as a moral imperative, and the American people responded. From 1948 to 1952, approximately 13 billion dollars in food, machinery and other aid products were sent across the Atlantic.

The time for big-thinking, bighearted American leadership is not over. The national government may be confused about its foreign policy objectives but the American Church is not. We have been clearly commanded by our King to go into all the world, preach the gospel and disciple the nations. The American passport, the English language, our level of prosperity and the ease of travel and communications has made it so easy for missionary enterprise to function. Our children are literally "going out to have a look" at potential mission fields before they choose the path of their college education.

Today's Christian leaders have led us out of bondage just as Moses did. We are no longer enslaved by deathly legalism or religiosity for its own sake. But a new wave is coming. It's time to cross the Jordan and inherit.

Brace yourself for the Joshua generation in missions; the best is yet to come.

■ ■ ■

21

SO WHAT
DO I DO?

Become a worshiper.

Have you ever been embarrassed in front of God?

"Jesus Christ!" came the angry curse. The couple behind me was beautiful, youthful and very loud. You could hear their complaint echo through the halls of the Canadian customs as the line of passengers inched toward the immigration booths.

The hardship they faced? Nothing really, only the inconvenience of one more connecting flight on the way home from a ski trip in Utah.

I bowed my head and apologized to God. All over the world God's character is maligned under the lash of accusing human tongues. It isn't fair. God has never made a selfish, unintelligent or unloving choice, yet His name is used as a common curse during petty inconvenience.

Jesus Himself should be the focus of the reconciler's heart.

Our essential motive in all this is to bring healing and joy to the broken heart of God. We seek the healing of America's wounds, not because America deserves healing, but because Jesus deserves to see the reward of the cross, the reconciliation of people to the Father and to each other.

Take the opportunity
of confession, with identification, when you find it.
Look at the circle of influence God has given you. For instance, through your job. If you have joined the U.S. Army, been elected to state office, joined the police department or become identified with any other vocation, you are an inheritor of its legacy and have become partly responsible for any unfinished business with God or offended persons.

> WE MUST BRING OUR OWN WOUNDED SPIRIT TO GOD IF WE ARE TO BE USED BY HIM AS RECONCILERS.

Don't miss the simple things that stem from your identity—as a mother, for instance. A lot of people's hurts center on an absent or dysfunctional mother. Sometimes a few humble words can begin a dramatic work of healing, even if there is no evidence of it at the time.

Release forgiveness and refrain from judgment.
We must bring our own wounded spirit to God if we are to be used by Him as reconcilers. All of us have experienced injustice. The obvious temptation of the offended person is to give in to self-pity; a feeling stemming from a deep inner vow that says, "I deserve better than this."

But do we? It is one thing to champion the rights of others; but do we ourselves really deserve better, in an absolute moral sense? I have often wallowed in self-pity but the truth is, the last thing I need is justice.

Justice cuts two ways. What if I really got what I deserve? I'm just another depraved human being with my own history of selfish actions. The fact is, I continue to live and breathe by the mercy of God; and having received mercy, I should extend mercy to others.

The righteousness I now live is by the power of the risen Christ, not the function of an informed intellect driven by the "milk" of human kindness. When I recognize my own desperate need for mercy, the gall of bitterness is more easily removed from my own spirit. When I acknowledge how much I have been forgiven, I am suddenly more able to release forgiveness toward those who have hurt me and mine.

The Bible sets an incredible standard for us in thought and speech. "[Love] bears all things, believes all things, hopes all things, endures all things" (1 Cor. 13:7). Racism and all the other prejudicial attitudes could be eradicated from the intercessor's heart if we simply give the other person, group or race the benefit of the doubt. Leave the judgment to God; refrain from coming to conclusions about the motives behind actions. Do not impute evil intent to any action that could be interpreted two ways. Suspicion and accusation have no place in the heart of the reconciler.

Receive God's gifts of friendship.
God organizes and builds His kingdom through gifts of friendship. As you follow principle and live out your particular obedience, God will call others to walk beside you from a diversity of backgrounds. Think again about the people God has put in your life; they're not just associates, God is up to something!

We live in a culture dominated by the ethos of trade. When we meet new people, we unconsciously calculate the advantage we can gain by the relationship. But that is not the way of the Kingdom. Jesus is ready to open our eyes to the beauty and value of the people around us. If we see with His eyes, we will soon follow the natural path from attraction to covenant.

Friendship is an eternal gift. All relationships are tested by difficulty from time to time, but our commitment should be to move toward one another rather than withdraw, to take up an ambition for one another's wholeness, empowerment and release into the full purpose of God.

Who is hanging out at the edges of your life right now? I know of many white believers who long for a black friend. I know immigrant families who would throw themselves into fellowship with Americans if shown the least hospitality. Yes there's awkwardness, yes it takes more work than just running with your own crowd, but the rewards are great. Let's go for it!

Join united efforts.
The local church, the gathering of believers, is the place where the concepts we have explored can be lived out most dynamically. That is why this book is addressed to the shepherds. Congregational life should be the cutting edge of positive change in American society.

We need sermons outlining the biblical basis for racial intermarriage. We need public confession and public reconciliation to take place in our sanctuaries on Sunday morning. We need to give place to the music of every people in our public worship. We have been in a soft-rock rut; listen, there is a new sound in the land. Let the performing arts flourish and give glory to God. Let the sounds of a huge, diverse nation ascend from our gathering.

Our denominational diversity provides another opportunity. The united Church is beginning to flow together like an irresistible tide. Through events such as March for Jesus, the

Church prophetically models the possibility of unity within a diversity on a citywide level. This also helps us, as individual believers, move beyond the tiny postage stamp of our own existence. We need to get involved in the prayer movements, missionary enterprises and mercy ministries of the Body of Christ in our cities. Whatever God has given you to do personally, do it with all your heart.

Volunteer help where America's pain is most evident.

My sister and brother-in-law are part of the network of agencies struggling to overcome AIDS in Los Angeles County. They minister in hospitals and hospices and even nurse patients in their own home until the patients die. An army of similar heros are already at work in your city. Find them, walk beside them and help them.

You will find like-minded people in the prayer movements such as Lydia or Intercessors for America. Attend neighborhood prayer meetings or citywide Concerts of Prayer. If solemn assemblies or reconciliation events are sponsored, be there. You will see nation-changing power released when believers move together in praise, repentance, intercession, spiritual warfare and the proclamation of blessing.

Look around.

Be an explorer. Let curiosity carry you far beyond the knowledge you now possess. Seek to understand the times and seasons as Daniel did. Seek to touch, know and celebrate the diversity of this nation. Ignorance is a curse. It will take an informed mind and an enlarged heart to embrace the ambition of God for the people of America.

Discern the Body of Christ.

What if I was to call you up front in a meeting and ask you a few questions? What if I threw at you the names of five or six denominations and ministries in your town and asked you to explain the redemptive purpose for each one? Could you do it?

We know who is out there, but we mostly know other movements through negative caricature—what's *wrong* with them. How they differ from *us*, the biblical ones. Is there an alternative to these prejudicial stereotypes?

While walking through a small town in Oklahoma, I came upon a somewhat dilapidated Methodist church. As I stood staring at the peeling paint, I remembered.

A feeling of reverential awe replaced my idol curiosity. I remembered that many of the circuit riders died in their 30s by drowning and disease, yet they kept coming. It was said that the second sound after the woodsman's axe on the frontier was the "Halloo!" of the Methodist preacher, announcing his arrival for meetings.

I remembered that this denomination, a uniquely American denomination, did more to shape the personality of the emerging nation than any other. It indirectly gave root to the renewal movements and revivalists of Pentecostalism and boosted the mercy ministries of groups such as the Salvation Army. "Lord, bless them!" I prayed. "May these people be revived and take their place on the walls of this city."

I glanced at my watch and made my way back to the motel. It was time to get ready for the conference I was attending at a thriving charismatic church nearby.

In my room, I happened to open my Bible to the book of Judges. The last few pages tell a scandalous story of sexual perversion, murder, dismemberment and conflict between Israel's tribes. The unrepentant depravity of Benjamin was putting all Israel at risk of God's judgment. In order to cleanse the land, the united tribes went to war against Benjamin, and at great cost the Benjamites were defeated. All that remained of this once mighty tribe were 600 fleet-footed young men, hiding in the wilderness.

The united Israelites suffered more than 40,000 casualties in the battle. In their anger and grief, the victorious tribes vowed to drive Benjamin into extinction by forbidding marriage with their daughters, and then the implications began to sink in. The Israelites gathered at Bethel weeping bitterly, not over their own loss but over the loss of a tribe. "And they said, 'There must be an inheritance for the survivors of Benjamin, that a tribe may not be blotted out from Israel'" (Judg. 21:17).

Do we have this attitude today? I think not. When a denomination becomes apostate, when a church down the street goes belly up, our attitude is often, "Good riddance! They were an embarrassment anyway. Nice building though; let's see if we can buy it."

Unlike most modern believers, the Israelites understood the role of a divinely ordained inheritance within the land. They understood the difference between Benjamin, depraved and apostate within their own generation, and Benjamin the dream in the heart of God.

Do you know the value of the movements and ministries in this nation? How can you encourage their potential if you remain ignorant of their story? The New Testament Greek word for truth, *aletheia*, means, "That which must not be forgotten."

Second Peter 3:1 says, "Stir up your pure minds by way of remembrance" *(KJV)*. It is as though the power to remember were an ethical principle, a form of righteous behavior.

When I meet that Salvation Army officer, or that Lutheran cleric, I want to provoke them to renewal by recounting their own heritage, not calling them to imitate mine. Let us give honor to all that is honorable and avoid that contentious spirit that makes absolutes out of what the Bible does not. Every missionary knows there is a great difference between form and meaning; that the cultural interpretation of biblical truth will vary, but the bedrock remains: an understanding of the nature, character and personality of God revealed through Jesus and His work. In addition to the foundational truths held by all the orthodox streams, there are the unique flashes of light shed by each. There is more than a division of labor in the Body of Christ. A division of emphasis also makes possible a wide view of a wide subject: God.

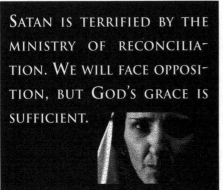

SATAN IS TERRIFIED BY THE MINISTRY OF RECONCILIATION. WE WILL FACE OPPOSITION, BUT GOD'S GRACE IS SUFFICIENT.

Hold your ground.
Satan is terrified by the ministry of reconciliation. We will face opposition, but God's grace is sufficient. Intense spiritual warfare has occurred during the writing of this book and the living of this life, but as I pen these final pages I see victory on every side.

At one point, my darling wife, Julie, was told she had a brain tumor; then the doctor mysteriously changed his mind—after prayer and further tests.

On another occasion, my oldest son was walking down the street near our home when he was jumped by five Latino men, forced to the ground and beaten with baseball bats. Fighting free he narrowly escaped abduction. He had just left a barrio birthday party attended by three of his friends, gang members who had turned to Christ just days before. Our van was stolen by local teens and wrecked for the second time. I was threatened by a white supremacist. And these are just the headlines.

The net result of all of this, strangely enough, is that we as a family all feel wonderfully protected. Good things keep happening. "Out of the eater came something to eat, and out of the strong came something sweet" (Judg. 14:14). It is a biblical truth that we always find some kind of provision in the midst of the enemy's attack.

My son is convinced that God delivered him from a fatal situation (many boys have died in our neighborhood), and at this writing he is in Calcutta, India, doing missionary work, obviously unintimidated by his experiences in Los Angeles.

The rest of our family is healthy and succeeding in our various tasks, and we have never felt so loved. The Holy Spirit has mobilized intercessors from all over the nation who seem to stand around us like a wall. We have been amazed at the way praying people call in, first describing exactly what we're going through, then encouraging us with the promises of God.

"A woman, when she is in labor, has sorrow because her hour has come; but as soon as she has given birth to the child, she no longer remembers the anguish, for joy that a human being has been born into the world" (John 16:21, *NKJV*).

Can you identify with that?

At this point in time, the American Church is in a sober season of travail, but our day of joy will come. Sustaining a stubborn hope is in itself an intercessory act. Look at Abraham:

> Who, contrary to hope, in hope believed, so that he became the father of many nations, according to what was spoken, "So shall your descendants be." And not being weak in faith, he did not consider his own body, already dead (since he was about a 100 years old), and the deadness of Sarah's womb. He did not waver at the promise of God through unbelief, but was strengthened in faith, giving glory to God (Rom. 4:18-20, *NKJV*).

Why would God delay the arrival of the child of promise? I think it was because the size of the baby determines the length of a pregnancy. (Consider the gestation period of an elephant — 20 to 22 months — as opposed to that of a field mouse — 18 to 21 days.)

I know that you yearn for a revival that seems long

delayed, but to the American Church I would say: **If you will not give up, God will use your faith to birth a multigenerational blessing out of the dead womb of today's circumstances.**

"O Israel, hope in the Lord. From this time forth and forever" (Ps. 131:3, *NKJV*).

It's Possible

I close this book as I began, looking at what's happening in New Zealand. Fresh in my memory are images that once existed only in my dreams.

October 1-4, 1993: The occasion was a kind of citywide party thrown by the Scripture in Song worship band on their 25th anniversary. They rented a stadium in Auckland and invited everybody. And everybody came, including a large contingent of Australian aborigines and native Hawaiians, plus many foreign guests.

This is the same worship band that anchored the citywide events back in 1990 when tears of repentance visited us during the 150th year celebrations. Now the mood was completely different. I still felt like crying, but for a different reason. Pure joy.

Maori elders were seated across a huge platform, representing the place of honor given to the host people of the land. The stadium floor was occupied by more than 20 people groups, each clustered in their native dress behind a banner proclaiming their identity.

In turn, each group came to the foot of the stage and was met by a Maori warrior in full battle regalia. The Maori way is to challenge a visitor to openly declare their intentions before safe passage into the tribal territory is granted. In this way, each people group reenacted its entry into New Zealand, except for one vital difference. This time they came as relatives claiming to be the offspring of the same father, the Creator of all things, the Most High God, the heavenly Father.

Each group asked for entry into the life of the nation, where appropriate, expressing sorrow over the sins of the past. After receiving a solemn welcome in Maori, each group lifted their voices in praise to God in their own language and, in preparation for a stadium-wide feast, placed gifts of food on the tables in front of the main stage until they were covered with ethnic breads and delicacies.

I sat on the platform transfixed by what I was seeing. They were re-laying the foundation of the land. They were tearing up the ancient root of conflict between races, the seed planted when Captain James Cook first landed among the Maoris in a tragic cross-cultural clash that left death and confusion. The landing was a fiasco that ended when Cook named the site "Poverty Bay" and sailed away, leaving that name like a curse forever branded on the geography of the nation.

Even more profound than this healing of old wounds was the emerging picture of the beauty of the peoples enriching the nation. Each people group poured out their praise to God in their native way until a new sound in the earth filled the great stadium. The ancient Hawaiian nose flute evoked the sound of the island winds. The throbbing drone of the didgeridoo captured the mystery of the desert night, and the exuberance of the Cook Island drums pulsed with the energy of living creation.

All around us there was praise; the voice of the peoples lifted to God, unmuffled by the old religious taboos.

I could see it clearly. The gifts within cultures. Japanese serenity, Samoan joy, Jewish revelation, Cook Island celebration, Chinese graciousness, European inclusion, Indian devotion, Tongan dignity, Malaysian artistry, Indonesian zeal, Hawaiian beauty and aboriginal endurance; and in the place of honor the beloved Maori, the unifying logo-type of the land. In the redeemed Maori is revealed the redemptive purpose for the nation as a whole. A nation generous in hospitality; eloquent in prophetic insight; with the vigor, strength and boldness of the warrior; and the protective gentleness of a mother with child.

This *can* happen, America. These are things I saw, rather than dreamed of; and every now and then I get a glimpse of God's plan for us, a prophetic Church, showing the way in the midst of modern America.

The Most Beautiful Sight in America

Dallas, Texas, hotel convention center: The whole stage is moving beneath me. Hundreds of choir members swing in unison, loosing layers of harmony in a torrent of ecstatic joy. Every last person in this auditorium is a vessel of praise, lost in happy celebration.

As a student of history and culture I can read the faces. I can see the diversity of the nations in the uplifted features — Africa and Asia, the Caribbean and the Northern steppes.

Against a backdrop of cascading sound and physical unison, musicians and a soloist step forward into the spotlight to lead us into new heights.

Completely lost to self-conscious sensitivities, rising above the memories of pain, we send a great wall of sound rising toward the throne of God.

Every eye is upturned. Every heart is straining within the limits of its earthen shell as the unspeakable joy of the rescued, the redeemed, ascends to the throne.

Lord, You have been faithful!
Lord, You have been faithful!
Lord, You have been faithful!
to me.

. . .

CONNECTIONS

MINISTRIES REFERRED TO IN THIS BOOK

1. **International Reconciliation Coalition**
   The International Reconciliation Coalition is a labor of love run by unsalaried volunteers and is supported by the donations of caring individuals.

   - **Founders Office** (books, tapes and materials)
     P.O. Box 296
     Sunland, CA 91041-0296
     Phone (818) 896-1589
     Fax (818) 896-2077

   - **International Office**
     Networking
     P.O. Box 471685
     San Francisco, CA 94147-1685
     Tel/Fax (415) 759-6630

   - **Native American Chapter of North America**
     P.O. Box 1417
     Castle Rock, CO 80104
     Phone (303) 660-9258
     Fax (303) 660-0621

2. **March for Jesus**
   USA National Office
   P.O. Box 3216
   Austin, TX 78764
   Phone (512) 416-0066
   Fax (512) 445-5393

3. **Youth With a Mission**
   Urban Missions
   P.O. Box 296
   Sunland, CA 91041-0296
   Phone (818) 896-1589
   Fax (818) 896-2077